FREE Test Taking Tips DVD Offer

To help us better serve you, we have developed a Test Taking Tips DVD that we would like to give you for FREE. **This DVD covers world-class test taking tips that you can use to be even more successful when you are taking your test.**

All that we ask is that you email us your feedback about your study guide. Please let us know what you thought about it – whether that is good, bad or indifferent.

To get your **FREE Test Taking Tips DVD**, email freedvd@studyguideteam.com with "FREE DVD" in the subject line and the following information in the body of the email:

a. The title of your study guide.

b. Your product rating on a scale of 1-5, with 5 being the highest rating.

c. Your feedback about the study guide. What did you think of it?

d. Your full name and shipping address to send your free DVD.

If you have any questions or concerns, please don't hesitate to contact us at freedvd@studyguideteam.com.

Thanks again!

SAT Math 1 Subject Test Prep
SAT Math Level 1 Study Guide

Test Prep Books

Table of Contents

Quick Overview

As you draw closer to taking your exam, effective preparation becomes more and more important. Thankfully, you have this study guide to help you get ready. Use this guide to help keep your studying on track and refer to it often.

This study guide contains several key sections that will help you be successful on your exam. The guide contains tips for what you should do the night before and the day of the test. Also included are test-taking tips. Knowing the right information is not always enough. Many well-prepared test takers struggle with exams. These tips will help equip you to accurately read, assess, and answer test questions.

A large part of the guide is devoted to showing you what content to expect on the exam and to helping you better understand that content. In this guide are practice test questions so that you can see how well you have grasped the content. Then, answer explanations are provided so that you can understand why you missed certain questions.

Don't try to cram the night before you take your exam. This is not a wise strategy for a few reasons. First, your retention of the information will be low. Your time would be better used by reviewing information you already know rather than trying to learn a lot of new information. Second, you will likely become stressed as you try to gain a large amount of knowledge in a short amount of time. Third, you will be depriving yourself of sleep. So be sure to go to bed at a reasonable time the night before. Being well-rested helps you focus and remain calm.

Be sure to eat a substantial breakfast the morning of the exam. If you are taking the exam in the afternoon, be sure to have a good lunch as well. Being hungry is distracting and can make it difficult to focus. You have hopefully spent lots of time preparing for the exam. Don't let an empty stomach get in the way of success!

When travelling to the testing center, leave earlier than needed. That way, you have a buffer in case you experience any delays. This will help you remain calm and will keep you from missing your appointment time at the testing center.

Be sure to pace yourself during the exam. Don't try to rush through the exam. There is no need to risk performing poorly on the exam just so you can leave the testing center early. Allow yourself to use all of the allotted time if needed.

Remain positive while taking the exam even if you feel like you are performing poorly. Thinking about the content you should have mastered will not help you perform better on the exam.

Once the exam is complete, take some time to relax. Even if you feel that you need to take the exam again, you will be well served by some down time before you begin studying again. It's often easier to convince yourself to study if you know that it will come with a reward!

Test-Taking Strategies

1. Predicting the Answer

When you feel confident in your preparation for a multiple-choice test, try predicting the answer before reading the answer choices. This is especially useful on questions that test objective factual knowledge. By predicting the answer before reading the available choices, you eliminate the possibility that you will be distracted or led astray by an incorrect answer choice. You will feel more confident in your selection if you read the question, predict the answer, and then find your prediction among the answer choices. After using this strategy, be sure to still read all of the answer choices carefully and completely. If you feel unprepared, you should not attempt to predict the answers. This would be a waste of time and an opportunity for your mind to wander in the wrong direction.

2. Reading the Whole Question

Too often, test takers scan a multiple-choice question, recognize a few familiar words, and immediately jump to the answer choices. Test authors are aware of this common impatience, and they will sometimes prey upon it. For instance, a test author might subtly turn the question into a negative, or he or she might redirect the focus of the question right at the end. The only way to avoid falling into these traps is to read the entirety of the question carefully before reading the answer choices.

3. Looking for Wrong Answers

Long and complicated multiple-choice questions can be intimidating. One way to simplify a difficult multiple-choice question is to eliminate all of the answer choices that are clearly wrong. In most sets of answers, there will be at least one selection that can be dismissed right away. If the test is administered on paper, the test taker could draw a line through it to indicate that it may be ignored; otherwise, the test taker will have to perform this operation mentally or on scratch paper. In either case, once the obviously incorrect answers have been eliminated, the remaining choices may be considered. Sometimes identifying the clearly wrong answers will give the test taker some information about the correct answer. For instance, if one of the remaining answer choices is a direct opposite of one of the eliminated answer choices, it may well be the correct answer. The opposite of obviously wrong is obviously right! Of course, this is not always the case. Some answers are obviously incorrect simply because they are irrelevant to the question being asked. Still, identifying and eliminating some incorrect answer choices is a good way to simplify a multiple-choice question.

4. Don't Overanalyze

Anxious test takers often overanalyze questions. When you are nervous, your brain will often run wild, causing you to make associations and discover clues that don't actually exist. If you feel that this may be a problem for you, do whatever you can to slow down during the test. Try taking a deep breath or counting to ten. As you read and consider the question, restrict yourself to the particular words used by the author. Avoid thought tangents about what the author *really* meant, or what he or she was *trying* to say. The only things that matter on a multiple-choice test are the words that are actually in the question. You must avoid reading too much into a multiple-choice question, or supposing that the writer meant something other than what he or she wrote.

5. No Need for Panic

It is wise to learn as many strategies as possible before taking a multiple-choice test, but it is likely that you will come across a few questions for which you simply don't know the answer. In this situation, avoid panicking. Because most multiple-choice tests include dozens of questions, the relative value of a single wrong answer is small. As much as possible, you should compartmentalize each question on a multiple-choice test. In other words, you should not allow your feelings about one question to affect your success on the others. When you find a question that you either don't understand or don't know how to answer, just take a deep breath and do your best. Read the entire question slowly and carefully. Try rephrasing the question a couple of different ways. Then, read all of the answer choices carefully. After eliminating obviously wrong answers, make a selection and move on to the next question.

6. Confusing Answer Choices

When working on a difficult multiple-choice question, there may be a tendency to focus on the answer choices that are the easiest to understand. Many people, whether consciously or not, gravitate to the answer choices that require the least concentration, knowledge, and memory. This is a mistake. When you come across an answer choice that is confusing, you should give it extra attention. A question might be confusing because you do not know the subject matter to which it refers. If this is the case, don't eliminate the answer before you have affirmatively settled on another. When you come across an answer choice of this type, set it aside as you look at the remaining choices. If you can confidently assert that one of the other choices is correct, you can leave the confusing answer aside. Otherwise, you will need to take a moment to try to better understand the confusing answer choice. Rephrasing is one way to tease out the sense of a confusing answer choice.

7. Your First Instinct

Many people struggle with multiple-choice tests because they overthink the questions. If you have studied sufficiently for the test, you should be prepared to trust your first instinct once you have carefully and completely read the question and all of the answer choices. There is a great deal of research suggesting that the mind can come to the correct conclusion very quickly once it has obtained all of the relevant information. At times, it may seem to you as if your intuition is working faster even than your reasoning mind. This may in fact be true. The knowledge you obtain while studying may be retrieved from your subconscious before you have a chance to work out the associations that support it. Verify your instinct by working out the reasons that it should be trusted.

8. Key Words

Many test takers struggle with multiple-choice questions because they have poor reading comprehension skills. Quickly reading and understanding a multiple-choice question requires a mixture of skill and experience. To help with this, try jotting down a few key words and phrases on a piece of scrap paper. Doing this concentrates the process of reading and forces the mind to weigh the relative importance of the question's parts. In selecting words and phrases to write down, the test taker thinks about the question more deeply and carefully. This is especially true for multiple-choice questions that are preceded by a long prompt.

9. Subtle Negatives

One of the oldest tricks in the multiple-choice test writer's book is to subtly reverse the meaning of a question with a word like *not* or *except*. If you are not paying attention to each word in the question, you can easily be led astray by this trick. For instance, a common question format is, "Which of the following is...?" Obviously, if the question instead is, "Which of the following is not...?," then the answer will be quite different. Even worse, the test makers are aware of the potential for this mistake and will include one answer choice that would be correct if the question were not negated or reversed. A test taker who misses the reversal will find what he or she believes to be a correct answer and will be so confident that he or she will fail to reread the question and discover the original error. The only way to avoid this is to practice a wide variety of multiple-choice questions and to pay close attention to each and every word.

10. Reading Every Answer Choice

It may seem obvious, but you should always read every one of the answer choices! Too many test takers fall into the habit of scanning the question and assuming that they understand the question because they recognize a few key words. From there, they pick the first answer choice that answers the question they believe they have read. Test takers who read all of the answer choices might discover that one of the latter answer choices is actually *more* correct. Moreover, reading all of the answer choices can remind you of facts related to the question that can help you arrive at the correct answer. Sometimes, a misstatement or incorrect detail in one of the latter answer choices will trigger your memory of the subject and will enable you to find the right answer. Failing to read all of the answer choices is like not reading all of the items on a restaurant menu: you might miss out on the perfect choice.

11. Spot the Hedges

One of the keys to success on multiple-choice tests is paying close attention to every word. This is never truer than with words like almost, most, some, and sometimes. These words are called "hedges" because they indicate that a statement is not totally true or not true in every place and time. An absolute statement will contain no hedges, but in many subjects, the answers are not always straightforward or absolute. There are always exceptions to the rules in these subjects. For this reason, you should favor those multiple-choice questions that contain hedging language. The presence of qualifying words indicates that the author is taking special care with his or her words, which is certainly important when composing the right answer. After all, there are many ways to be wrong, but there is only one way to be right! For this reason, it is wise to avoid answers that are absolute when taking a multiple-choice test. An absolute answer is one that says things are either all one way or all another. They often include words like *every*, *always*, *best*, and *never*. If you are taking a multiple-choice test in a subject that doesn't lend itself to absolute answers, be on your guard if you see any of these words.

12. Long Answers

In many subject areas, the answers are not simple. As already mentioned, the right answer often requires hedges. Another common feature of the answers to a complex or subjective question are qualifying clauses, which are groups of words that subtly modify the meaning of the sentence. If the question or answer choice describes a rule to which there are exceptions or the subject matter is complicated, ambiguous, or confusing, the correct answer will require many words in order to be expressed clearly and accurately. In essence, you should not be deterred by answer choices that seem excessively long. Oftentimes, the author of the text will not be able to write the correct answer without offering some qualifications and modifications. Your job is to read the answer choices thoroughly and completely and to select the one that most accurately and precisely answers the question.

13. Restating to Understand

Sometimes, a question on a multiple-choice test is difficult not because of what it asks but because of how it is written. If this is the case, restate the question or answer choice in different words. This process serves a couple of important purposes. First, it forces you to concentrate on the core of the question. In order to rephrase the question accurately, you have to understand it well. Rephrasing the question will concentrate your mind on the key words and ideas. Second, it will present the information to your mind in a fresh way. This process may trigger your memory and render some useful scrap of information picked up while studying.

14. True Statements

Sometimes an answer choice will be true in itself, but it does not answer the question. This is one of the main reasons why it is essential to read the question carefully and completely before proceeding to the answer choices. Too often, test takers skip ahead to the answer choices and look for true statements. Having found one of these, they are content to select it without reference to the question above. Obviously, this provides an easy way for test makers to play tricks. The savvy test taker will always read the entire question before turning to the answer choices. Then, having settled on a correct answer choice, he or she will refer to the original question and ensure that the selected answer is relevant. The mistake of choosing a correct-but-irrelevant answer choice is especially common on questions related to specific pieces of objective knowledge. A prepared test taker will have a wealth of factual knowledge at his or her disposal, and should not be careless in its application.

15. No Patterns

One of the more dangerous ideas that circulates about multiple-choice tests is that the correct answers tend to fall into patterns. These erroneous ideas range from a belief that B and C are the most common right answers, to the idea that an unprepared test-taker should answer "A-B-A-C-A-D-A-B-A." It cannot be emphasized enough that pattern-seeking of this type is exactly the WRONG way to approach a multiple-choice test. To begin with, it is highly unlikely that the test maker will plot the correct answers according to some predetermined pattern. The questions are scrambled and delivered in a random order. Furthermore, even if the test maker was following a pattern in the assignation of correct answers, there is no reason why the test taker would know which pattern he or she was using. Any attempt to discern a pattern in the answer choices is a waste of time and a distraction from the real work of taking the test. A test taker would be much better served by extra preparation before the test than by reliance on a pattern in the answers.

FREE DVD OFFER

Don't forget that doing well on your exam includes both understanding the test content and understanding how to use what you know to do well on the test. We offer a completely FREE Test Taking Tips DVD that covers world class test taking tips that you can use to be even more successful when you are taking your test.

All that we ask is that you email us your feedback about your study guide. To get your **FREE Test Taking Tips DVD**, email freedvd@studyguideteam.com with "FREE DVD" in the subject line and the following information in the body of the email:

- The title of your study guide.
- Your product rating on a scale of 1-5, with 5 being the highest rating.
- Your feedback about the study guide. What did you think of it?
- Your full name and shipping address to send your free DVD.

Introduction

Function of the Test

The Mathematics Level 1 Subject Test is a test that examines your knowledge of geometry and algebra in order to showcase your abilities to college admissions programs. Some colleges use Mathematics 1 to place students in appropriate courses in college, allowing them to pass over the basics into more complex courses. Note that in New York State, some people may use SAT Subject Test scores as a substitute for a Regents examination score. The Mathematics Level 1 Subject Test examines your knowledge of mathematics within a two-year period of algebra and a one-year period of geometry.

Test Administration

To find out where the Mathematics Level 1 Subject Test is given, go to the website at collegereadiness.collegeboard.org. There you can find exam dates for the current year as well as up to three years in advance. The dates are listed by subject and give a deadline to register for each date. Currently, there are six dates listed each year for taking the subject tests, all of which offer the Mathematics 1 subject test. The dates for the exams are offered in August, October, November, December, May, and June. Note that you cannot take the SAT and an SAT Subject Test on the same date. The College Board website also has a test date finder, where you enter in the test date and your country, state, and city. The results bring up testing centers in your area or the area(s) nearest you.

Test Format

The Mathematics Level 1 Subject test is sixty minutes long and has fifty multiple choice questions. The skills that are needed in order to be successful on the exam are numbers and operations; algebra and functions; geometry and measurement; and statistics, probability, and data analysis. The test sections are divided according to percentages in the table below:

Content	Percentage
Number and operations	10 to 14%
Algebra and functions	38 to 42%
Geometry and measurement	38 to 42%
Data analysis, statistics and probability	8 to 12%

Note that the difference between Mathematics 1 and Mathematics 2 is that Mathematics 2 is for test takers who are adept in the subjects of trigonometry or precalculus and know how to use a graphing calculator. In order to decide between the two tests, take a look at which subjects you are recently familiar with and what college programs you are most interested in.

Test takers are allowed to bring calculators for the exam day. Keep in mind that many of the answer choices on the Mathematics 1 exam are rounded, so the calculator answer may not be the exact answer choice you see on the exam. Remember to read each problem carefully and to not jump at the very first number that matches an answer choice. Follow the question through to the end.

Scoring

In 2016, 66,058 students took the Mathematics Level 1 Subject Test. Out of a 200 to 800-point scale, the mean score was 599. The standard deviation was 116; this calculates the spread of grades around the average score. A "good score" for the Mathematics Level 1 Subject Test depends on the college you are applying to. Although many colleges are flexible and look at SAT scores along with other factors for admissions, highly selective schools prefer to see a score in the 700s or above. Note that you do not have to take SAT Subject Tests for admission to most colleges; even many highly selective schools recommend but do not require the exam.

Recent Developments

The only new developments for the subject tests are changes to the testing calendar. A new test date is offered on Saturday, August 26, 2017. For students who have to miss the Saturday test for religious reasons, the test is also offered on Sunday, August 27. Exam dates are no longer offered in January. March testing is available internationally, and subject tests will be offered outside of the U.S. and U.S. territories in October, November, December, May, and June.

Number and Operations

Structure of the Number System

The mathematical number system is made up of two general types of numbers: real and complex. *Real numbers* are those that are used in normal settings, while *complex numbers* are those composed of both a real number and an imaginary one. Imaginary numbers are the result of taking the square root of -1, and $\sqrt{-1} = i$.

The real number system is often explained using a Venn diagram similar to the one below. After a number has been labeled as a real number, further classification occurs when considering the other groups in this diagram. If a number is a never-ending, non-repeating decimal, it falls in the irrational category. Otherwise, it is rational. More information on these types of numbers is provided in the previous section. Furthermore, if a number does not have a fractional part, it is classified as an integer, such as -2, 75, or zero. Whole numbers are an even smaller group that only includes positive integers and zero. The last group of natural numbers is made up of only positive integers, such as 2, 56, or 12.

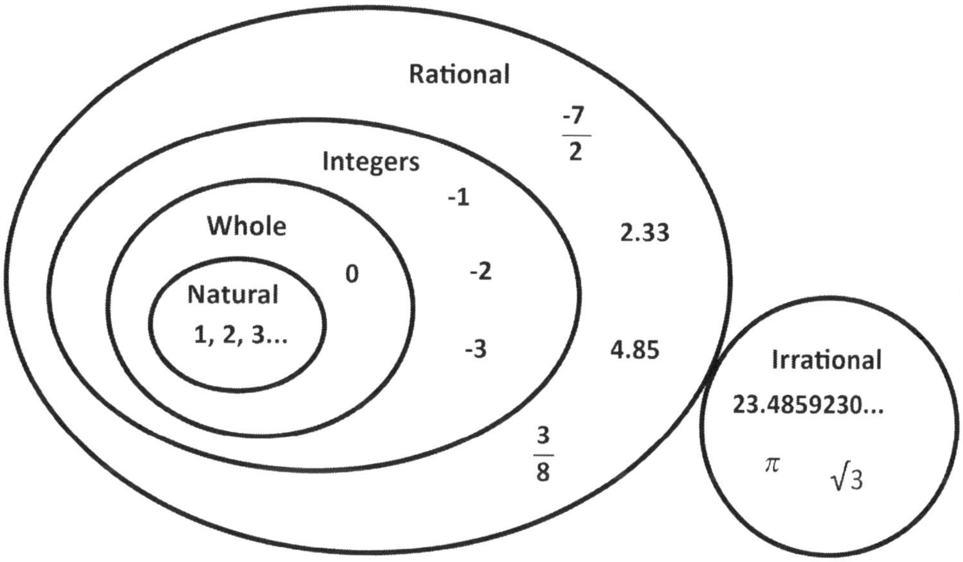

Real numbers can be compared and ordered using the number line. If a number falls to the left on the real number line, it is less than a number on the right. For example, $-2 < 5$ because -2 falls to the left of zero, and 5 falls to the right. Numbers to the left of zero are negative while those to the right are positive.

Complex numbers are made up of the sum of a real number and an imaginary number. Some examples of complex numbers include $6 + 2i$, $5 - 7i$, and $-3 + 12i$. Adding and subtracting complex numbers is similar to collecting like terms. The real numbers are added together, and the imaginary numbers are added together. For example, if the problem asks to simplify the expression $6 + 2i - 3 + 7i$, the 6 and -3 are combined to make 3, and the $2i$ and $7i$ combine to make $9i$. Multiplying and dividing complex numbers is similar to working with exponents. One rule to remember when multiplying is that $i * i = -1$. For example, if a problem asks to simplify the expression $4i(3 + 7i)$, the $4i$ should be distributed throughout the 3 and the $7i$. This leaves the final expression $12i - 28$. The 28 is negative because $i * i$

results in a negative number. The last type of operation to consider with complex numbers is the conjugate. The *conjugate* of a complex number is a technique used to change the complex number into a real number. For example, the conjugate of $4 - 3i$ is $4 + 3i$. Multiplying $(4 - 3i)(4 + 3i)$ results in $16 + 12i - 12i + 9$, which has a final answer of $16 + 9 = 25$.

The order of operations—PEMDAS—simplifies longer expressions with real or imaginary numbers. Each operation is listed in the order of how they should be completed in a problem containing more than one operation. Parentheses can also mean grouping symbols, such as brackets and absolute value. Then, exponents are calculated. Multiplication and division should be completed from left to right, and addition and subtraction should be completed from left to right.

Simplification of another type of expression occurs when radicals are involved. As explained previously, root is another word for radical. For example, the following expression is a radical that can be simplified: $\sqrt{24x^2}$. First, the number must be factored out to the highest perfect square. Any perfect square can be taken out of a radical. Twenty-four can be factored into 4 and 6, and 4 can be taken out of the radical. $\sqrt{4} = 2$ can be taken out, and 6 stays underneath. If $x > 0$, x can be taken out of the radical because it is a perfect square. The simplified radical is $2x\sqrt{6}$. An approximation can be found using a calculator.

There are also properties of numbers that are true for certain operations. The *commutative* property allows the order of the terms in an expression to change while keeping the same final answer. Both addition and multiplication can be completed in any order and still obtain the same result. However, order does matter in subtraction and division. The *associative* property allows any terms to be "associated" by parenthesis and retain the same final answer. For example, $(4 + 3) + 5 = 4 + (3 + 5)$. Both addition and multiplication are associative; however, subtraction and division do not hold this property. The *distributive* property states that $a(b + c) = ab + ac$. It is a property that involves both addition and multiplication, and the *a* is distributed onto each term inside the parentheses.

Integers can be factored into prime numbers. To *factor* is to express as a product. For example, $6 = 3 \cdot 2$, and $6 = 6 \cdot 1$. Both are factorizations, but the expression involving the factors of 3 and 2 is known as a *prime factorization* because it is factored into a product of two *prime numbers*—integers which do not have any factors other than themselves and 1. A *composite number* is a positive integer that can be divided into at least one other integer other than itself and 1, such as 6. Integers that have a factor of 2 are even, and if they are not divisible by 2, they are odd. Finally, a *multiple* of a number is the product of that number and a counting number—also known as a *natural number*. For example, some multiples of 4 are 4, 8, 12, 16, etc.

Basic Operations of Arithmetic

There are four different basic operations used with numbers: addition, subtraction, multiplication, and division.

- Addition takes two numbers and combines them into a total called the sum. The sum is the total when combining two collections into one. If there are 5 things in one collection and 3 in another, then after combining them, there is a total of $5 + 3 = 8$. Note the order does not matter when adding numbers. For example, $3 + 5 = 8$.

- Subtraction is the opposite (or "inverse") operation to addition. Whereas addition combines two quantities together, subtraction takes one quantity away from another. For example, if there are 20 gallons of fuel and 5 are removed, that gives $20 - 5 = 15$ gallons remaining. Note that for subtraction, the order does matter because it makes a difference which quantity is being removed from which.

- Multiplication is repeated addition. 3×4 can be thought of as putting together 3 sets of items, each set containing 4 items. The total is 12 items. Another way to think of this is to think of each number as the length of one side of a rectangle. If a rectangle is covered in tiles with 3 columns of 4 tiles each, then there are 12 tiles in total. From this, one can see that the answer is the same if the rectangle has 4 rows of 3 tiles each: $4 \times 3 = 12$. By expanding this reasoning, the order the numbers are multiplied does not matter.

- Division is the opposite of multiplication. It means taking one quantity and dividing it into sets the size of the second quantity. If there are 16 sandwiches to be distributed to 4 people, then each person gets $16 \div 4 = 4$ sandwiches. As with subtraction, the order in which the numbers appear does matter for division.

Addition

Addition is the combination of two numbers so their quantities are added together cumulatively. The sign for an addition operation is the + symbol. For example, 9 + 6 = 15. The 9 and 6 combine to achieve a cumulative value, called a sum.

Addition holds the commutative property, which means that numbers in an addition equation can be switched without altering the result. The formula for the commutative property is a + b = b + a. Let's look at a few examples to see how the commutative property works:

$$7 = 3 + 4 = 4 + 3 = 7$$

$$20 = 12 + 8 = 8 + 12 = 20$$

Addition also holds the associative property, which means that the grouping of numbers doesn't matter in an addition problem. In other words, the presence or absence of parentheses is irrelevant. The formula for the associative property is $(a + b) + c = a + (b + c)$. Here are some examples of the associative property at work:

$$30 = (6 + 14) + 10 = 6 + (14 + 10) = 30$$

$$35 = 8 + (2 + 25) = (8 + 2) + 25 = 35$$

Subtraction

Subtraction is taking away one number from another, so their quantities are reduced. The sign designating a subtraction operation is the – symbol, and the result is called the difference. For example, $9 - 6 = 3$. The number *6* detracts from the number *9* to reach the difference *3*.

Unlike addition, subtraction follows neither the commutative nor associative properties. The order and grouping in subtraction impact the result.

$$15 = 22 - 7 \neq 7 - 22 = -15$$

$$3 = (10 - 5) - 2 \neq 10 - (5 - 2) = 7$$

When working through subtraction problems involving larger numbers, it's necessary to regroup the numbers. Let's work through a practice problem using regrouping:

$$\begin{array}{r} 3\ 2\ 5 \\ -\ \ 7\ 7 \\ \hline \end{array}$$

Here, it is clear that the ones and tens columns for 77 are greater than the ones and tens columns for 325. To subtract this number, borrow from the tens and hundreds columns. When borrowing from a column, subtracting 1 from the lender column will add 10 to the borrower column:

$$\begin{array}{lcc} 3\text{-}1 & 10\text{+}2\text{-}1 & 10\text{+}5 \\ - & 7 & 7 \\ \hline \end{array} = \begin{array}{lrr} 2 & 11 & 15 \\ - & 7 & 7 \\ \hline & 2\ \ 4 & 8 \end{array}$$

After ensuring that each digit in the top row is greater than the digit in the corresponding bottom row, subtraction can proceed as normal, and the answer is found to be 248.

Multiplication

Multiplication involves adding together multiple copies of a number. It is indicated by an $\times$ symbol or a number immediately outside of a parenthesis. For example:

$$5(8-2)$$

The two numbers being multiplied together are called factors, and their result is called a product. For example, $9 \times 6 = 54$. This can be shown alternatively by expansion of either the 9 or the 6:

$$9 \times 6 = 9 + 9 + 9 + 9 + 9 + 9 = 54$$

$$9 \times 6 = 6 + 6 + 6 + 6 + 6 + 6 + 6 + 6 + 6 = 54$$

Like addition, multiplication holds the commutative and associative properties:

$$115 = 23 \times 5 = 5 \times 23 = 115$$

$$84 = 3 \times (7 \times 4) = (3 \times 7) \times 4 = 84$$

Multiplication also follows the distributive property, which allows the multiplication to be distributed through parentheses. The formula for distribution is $a \times (b + c) = ab + ac$. This is clear after the examples:

$$45 = 5 \times 9 = 5(3 + 6) = (5 \times 3) + (5 \times 6) = 15 + 30 = 45$$

$$20 = 4 \times 5 = 4(10 - 5) = (4 \times 10) - (4 \times 5) = 40 - 20 = 20$$

Multiplication becomes slightly more complicated when multiplying numbers with decimals. The easiest way to answer these problems is to ignore the decimals and multiply as if they were whole numbers. After multiplying the factors, place a decimal in the product. The placement of the decimal is determined by taking the cumulative number of decimal places in the factors.

For example:

0.7	2.6	1.5
x 3	x 4.2	x 6.4
2.1	10.92	9.60

Let's tackle the first example. First, ignore the decimal and multiply the numbers as though they were whole numbers to arrive at a product: 21. Second, count the number of digits that follow a decimal (one). Finally, move the decimal place that many positions to the left, as the factors have only one decimal place. The second example works the same way, except that there are two total decimal places in the factors, so the product's decimal is moved two places over. In the third example, the decimal should be moved over two digits, but the digit zero is no longer needed, so it is erased and the final answer is 9.6.

Division

Division and multiplication are inverses of each other in the same way that addition and subtraction are opposites. The signs designating a division operation are the ÷ and / symbols. In division, the second number divides into the first.

The number before the division sign is called the dividend or, if expressed as a fraction, the numerator. For example, in $a \div b$, a is the dividend, while in $\frac{a}{b}$, a is the numerator.

The number after the division sign is called the divisor or, if expressed as a fraction, the denominator. For example, in $a \div b$, b is the divisor, while in $\frac{a}{b}$, b is the denominator.

Like subtraction, division doesn't follow the commutative property, as it matters which number comes before the division sign, and division doesn't follow the associative or distributive properties for the same reason.

For example:

$$\frac{3}{2} = 9 \div 6 \neq 6 \div 9 = \frac{2}{3}$$

$$2 = 10 \div 5 = (30 \div 3) \div 5 \neq 30 \div (3 \div 5) = 30 \div \frac{3}{5} = 50$$

$$25 = 20 + 5 = (40 \div 2) + (40 \div 8) \neq 40 \div (2 + 8) = 40 \div 10 = 4$$

If a divisor doesn't divide into a dividend an integer number of times, whatever is left over is termed the remainder. The remainder can be further divided out into decimal form by using long division; however, this doesn't always give a quotient with a finite number of decimal places, so the remainder can also be expressed as a fraction over the original divisor.

Division with decimals is similar to multiplication with decimals in that when dividing a decimal by a whole number, ignore the decimal and divide as if it were a whole number.

Upon finding the answer, or quotient, place the decimal at the decimal place equal to that in the dividend.

$$15.75 \div 3 = 5.25$$

When the divisor is a decimal number, multiply both the divisor and dividend by 10. Repeat this until the divisor is a whole number, then complete the division operation as described above.

$$\mathbf{17.5 \div 2.5 = 175 \div 25 = 7}$$

Order of Operations

When working with complicated expressions, parentheses are used to indicate in which order to perform operations. However, to avoid having too many parentheses in an expression, here are some basic rules concerning the proper order to perform operations when not otherwise specified.

1. Parentheses: always perform operations inside parentheses first, regardless of what those operations are
2. Exponents
3. Multiplication and Division
4. Addition and Subtraction

For #3 & #4, work these from left to right. So, if there a subtraction problem and then an addition problem, the subtraction problem will be worked first.

Note that multiplication and division are performed from left to right as they appear in the expression or equation. Addition and subtraction also are performed from left to right as they appear.

As an aid to memorizing this, some students like to use the mnemonic PEMDAS. Furthermore, this acronym can be associated with a mnemonic phrase such as "Pirates Eat Many Donuts At Sea."

Ratios and Proportions

Ratios are used to show the relationship between two quantities. The ratio of oranges to apples in the grocery store may be 3 to 2. That means that for every 3 oranges, there are 2 apples. This comparison can be expanded to represent the actual number of oranges and apples. Another example may be the number of boys to girls in a math class. If the ratio of boys to girls is given as 2 to 5, that means there are 2 boys to every 5 girls in the class. Ratios can also be compared if the units in each ratio are the same. The ratio of boys to girls in the math class can be compared to the ratio of boys to girls in a science class by stating which ratio is higher and which is lower.

Rates are used to compare two quantities with different units. *Unit rates* are the simplest form of rate. With unit rates, the denominator in the comparison of two units is one. For example, if someone can type at a rate of 1000 words in 5 minutes, then his or her unit rate for typing is $\frac{1000}{5} = 200$ words in one minute or 200 words per minute. Any rate can be converted into a unit rate by dividing to make the denominator one. 1000 words in 5 minutes has been converted into the unit rate of 200 words per minute.

Ratios and rates can be used together to convert rates into different units. For example, if someone is driving 50 kilometers per hour, that rate can be converted into miles per hour by using a ratio known as the *conversion factor*. Since the given value contains kilometers and the final answer needs to be in miles, the ratio relating miles to kilometers needs to be used. There are 0.62 miles in 1 kilometer. This, written as a ratio and in fraction form, is:

$$\frac{0.62\ miles}{1\ km}$$

To convert 50km/hour into miles per hour, the following conversion needs to be set up:

$$\frac{50\ km}{hour} * \frac{0.62\ miles}{1\ km} = 31\ miles\ per\ hour$$

The ratio between two similar geometric figures is called the *scale factor*. For example, a problem may depict two similar triangles, A and B. The scale factor from the smaller triangle A to the larger triangle B is given as 2 because the length of the corresponding side of the larger triangle, 16, is twice the corresponding side on the smaller triangle, 8. This scale factor can also be used to find the value of a missing side, x, in triangle A. Since the scale factor from the smaller triangle (A) to larger one (B) is 2, the larger corresponding side in triangle B (given as 25), can be divided by 2 to find the missing side in A (x = 12.5). The scale factor can also be represented in the equation $2A = B$ because two times the lengths of A gives the corresponding lengths of B. This is the idea behind similar triangles.

Much like a scale factor can be written using an equation like $2A = B$, a *relationship* is represented by the equation $Y = kX$. X and Y are proportional because as values of X increase, the values of Y also increase. A relationship that is inversely proportional can be represented by the equation $Y = \frac{k}{X}$, where the value of Y decreases as the value of x increases and vice versa.

Proportional reasoning can be used to solve problems involving ratios, percentages, and averages. Ratios can be used in setting up proportions and solving them to find unknowns. For example, if a student completes an average of 10 pages of math homework in 3 nights, how long would it take the student to complete 22 pages? Both ratios can be written as fractions. The second ratio would contain the unknown.

The following proportion represents this problem, where x is the unknown number of nights:

$$\frac{10\,pages}{3\,nights} = \frac{22\,pages}{x\,nights}$$

Solving this proportion entails cross-multiplying and results in the following equation: $10x = 22 * 3$. Simplifying and solving for x results in the exact solution: $x = 6.6\,nights$. The result would be rounded up to 7 because the homework would actually be completed on the 7th night.

The following problem uses ratios involving percentages:

> If 20% of the class is girls and 30 students are in the class, how many girls are in the class?

To set up this problem, it is helpful to use the common proportion:

$$\frac{\%}{100} = \frac{is}{of}$$

Within the proportion, % is the percentage of girls, 100 is the total percentage of the class, *is* is the number of girls, and *of* is the total number of students in the class. Most percentage problems can be written using this language. To solve this problem, the proportion should be set up as $\frac{20}{100} = \frac{x}{30}$, and then solved for x. Cross-multiplying results in the equation $20 * 30 = 100x$, which results in the solution $x = 6$. There are 6 girls in the class.

Problems involving volume, length, and other units can also be solved using ratios. A problem may ask for the volume of a cone to be found that has a radius, $r = 7m$ and a height, $h = 16m$. Referring to the formulas provided on the test, the volume of a cone is given as:

$$V = \pi r^2 \frac{h}{3}$$

r is the radius, and h is the height. Plugging $r = 7$ and $h = 16$ into the formula, the following is obtained:

$$V = \pi(7^2)\frac{16}{3}$$

Therefore, volume of the cone is found to be approximately 821m^3. Sometimes, answers in different units are sought. If this problem wanted the answer in liters, 821m^3 would need to be converted.

Using the equivalence statement $1\text{m}^3 = 1000\text{L}$, the following ratio would be used to solve for liters:

$$821\text{m}^3 * \frac{1000L}{1m^3}$$

Cubic meters in the numerator and denominator cancel each other out, and the answer is converted to 821,000 liters, or $8.21 * 10^5$ L.

Other conversions can also be made between different given and final units. If the temperature in a pool is 30°C, what is the temperature of the pool in degrees Fahrenheit? To convert these units, an equation is used relating Celsius to Fahrenheit. The following equation is used:

$$T_{°F} = 1.8T_{°C} + 32$$

Plugging in the given temperature and solving the equation for T yields the result:

$$T_{°F} = 1.8(30) + 32 = 86°F$$

Both units in the metric system and U.S. customary system are widely used.

Complex Numbers

Some types of equations can be solved to find real answers, but this is not the case for all equations. For example, $x^2 = k$ can be solved when *k* is non-negative, but it has no real solutions when *k* is negative. Equations do have solutions if complex numbers are allowed.

Complex numbers are defined in the following manner: every complex number can be written as $a + bi$, where $i^2 = -1$. Thus, the solutions to the equation $x^2 = -1$ are $\pm i$.

In order to find roots of negative numbers more generally, the properties of roots (or of exponents) are used. For example, $\sqrt{-4} = \sqrt{-1}\sqrt{4} = \pm 2i$. All arithmetic operations can be performed with complex numbers, where i is like any other constant. The value of i^2 can replace -1.

Matrices

Matrices can be used to represent linear equations, solve systems of equations, and manipulate data to simulate change. Matrices consist of numerical entries in both rows and columns. The following matrix A is a $3\ x\ 4$ matrix because it has three rows and four columns:

$$A = \begin{bmatrix} 3 & 2 & -5 & 3 \\ 3 & 6 & 2 & -5 \\ -1 & 3 & 7 & 0 \end{bmatrix}$$

Matrices can be added or subtracted only if they have the same dimensions. For example, the following matrices can be added by adding corresponding matrix entries:

$$\begin{bmatrix} 3 & 4 \\ 2 & -6 \end{bmatrix} + \begin{bmatrix} -1 & 4 \\ 4 & 2 \end{bmatrix} = \begin{bmatrix} 2 & 8 \\ 6 & -4 \end{bmatrix}$$

Multiplication can also be used to manipulate matrices. *Scalar multiplication* involves multiplying a matrix by a constant. Each matrix entry needs to be multiplied times the constant. The following example shows a $3\ x\ 2$ matrix being multiplied by the constant 6:

$$6 * \begin{bmatrix} 3 & 4 \\ 2 & -6 \\ 1 & 0 \end{bmatrix} = \begin{bmatrix} 18 & 24 \\ 12 & -36 \\ 6 & 0 \end{bmatrix}$$

Matrix multiplication of two matrices involves finding multiple dot products. The *dot product* of a row and column is the sum of the products of each corresponding row and column entry. In the following example, a $2\ x\ 2$ matrix is multiplied by a $2\ x\ 2$ matrix. The dot product of the first row and column is:

$$(1 * 2) + (2 * 1) = (2) + (2) = 4$$

$$\begin{bmatrix} 1 & 2 \\ 3 & 4 \end{bmatrix} \text{X} \begin{bmatrix} 2 & 0 \\ 1 & 2 \end{bmatrix} = \begin{bmatrix} 4 & 4 \\ 10 & 8 \end{bmatrix}$$

The same process is followed to find the other three values in the solution matrix. Matrices can only be multiplied if the number of columns in the first matrix equals the number of rows in the second matrix. The previous example is also an example of square matrix multiplication because they are both square matrices. A *square matrix* has the same number of rows and columns. For square matrices, the order in which they are multiplied does matter. Therefore, matrix multiplication does not satisfy the commutative property. It does, however, satisfy the associative and distributive properties.

Another transformation of matrices can be found by using the *identity matrix*—also referred to as the "I" matrix. The identity matrix is similar to the number one in normal multiplication. The identity matrix is a square matrix with ones in the diagonal spots and zeros everywhere else. The identity matrix is also the result of multiplying a matrix by its inverse. This process is similar to multiplying a number by its reciprocal.

The *zero matrix* is also a matrix acting as an additive identity. The zero matrix consists of zeros in every entry. It does not change the values of a matrix when using addition.

Given a system of linear equations, a matrix can be used to represent the entire system. Operations can then be performed on the matrix to solve the system. The following system offers an example:

$$\begin{aligned} x + y + z &= 6 \\ y + 5z &= -4 \\ 2x + 5y - z &= 27 \end{aligned}$$

There are three variables and three equations. The coefficients in the equations can be used to form a 3 x 3 matrix:

$$\begin{bmatrix} 1 & 1 & 1 \\ 0 & 1 & 5 \\ 2 & 5 & -1 \end{bmatrix}$$

The number of rows equals the number of equations, and the number of columns equals the number of variables. The numbers on the right side of the equations can be turned into a 3 x 1 matrix. That matrix is shown here:

$$\begin{bmatrix} 6 \\ -4 \\ 27 \end{bmatrix}$$

It can also be referred to as a *vector*. The variables are represented in a matrix of their own:

$$\begin{bmatrix} x \\ y \\ z \end{bmatrix}$$

The system can be represented by the following matrix equation:

$$\begin{bmatrix} 1 & 1 & 1 \\ 0 & 2 & 5 \\ 2 & 5 & -1 \end{bmatrix}\begin{bmatrix} x \\ y \\ z \end{bmatrix}=\begin{bmatrix} 6 \\ -4 \\ 27 \end{bmatrix}$$

Simply, this is written as $AX = B$. By using the inverse of a matrix, the solution can be found: $X = A^{-1}B$. Once the inverse of A is found using operations, it is then multiplied by B to find the solution to the system: $x = 5, y = 3, \text{and } z = -2$.

The determinant of a 2 x 2 matrix is the following:

$$|A| = \begin{vmatrix} a & b \\ c & d \end{vmatrix} = ad - bc$$

It is a number related to the size of the matrix. The absolute value of the determinant of matrix A is equal to the area of a parallelogram with vertices (0, 0), (a, b), (c, d), and (a+b, c+d).

Sequences and Series

A *sequence* is an enumerated set of numbers, and each term or member is defined by the number that exists within the sequence. It can have either a finite or infinite number of terms, and a sequence is written as $\{a_n\}$, where a_n is the nth term of the sequence. An example of an infinite sequence is:

$$\left\{\frac{n+1}{n^2}\right\}_{n=1}^{\infty}$$

Its first three terms are found by evaluating at n=1, 2, and 3 to get 2, $\frac{3}{4}$, and $\frac{4}{9}$. Limits of infinite sequences, if they exist, can be found in a similar manner as finding infinite limits of functions. n needs to be treated as a variable, and then $\lim_{n\to\infty} \frac{n+1}{n^2}$ can be evaluated, resulting in 0.

An infinite series is the sum of an infinite sequence. For example, $\sum_{n=1}^{\infty} \frac{n+1}{n^2}$ is the infinite series of the sequence given above. Partial sums are sums of a finite number of terms. For example, s_{10} represents the sum of the first 10 terms, and in general, s_n represents the sum of the first n terms. An infinite series can either converge or diverge. If the sum of an infinite series is a finite number, the series is said to *converge*. Otherwise, it *diverges*. In the general infinite series $\sum a_n$, If $\lim_{n\to\infty} a_n \neq 0$ or does not exist, the series diverges. However, if $\lim_{n\to\infty} a_n = 0$, the series does not necessarily converge.

Several tests exist that determine whether a series converges:

- The Absolute Convergence Test states that if $\sum |a_n|$ converges, then $\sum a_n$ converges.
- The Integral Test states that if $f(n) = a_n$ is a positive, continuous, decreasing function, then $\sum a_n$ is convergent if and only if $\int_1^\infty f(x)dx$ is convergent. The geometric series $\sum ar^{n-1}$ is convergent if $|r| < 1$ and its sum is equal to $\frac{a}{1-r}$. If $|r| \geq 1$, the geometric series is divergent.
- The Limit Comparison Tests compares two infinite series $\sum a_n$ and $\sum b_n$ with positive terms. If $\sum b_n$converges and $a_n \leq b_n$ for all n, then $\sum a_n$ converges. If $\sum b_n$diverges and $a_n \geq b_n$for all n, then $\sum a_n$ diverges. If $\lim_{n\to\infty} \frac{a_n}{b_n} = c$, where c is a finite, positive number, then either both series converge or diverge.
- The Alternating Series Test states that if $b_{n+1} \geq b_n$ for all n and $\lim_{n\to\infty} b_n = 0$, then the series $\sum(-1)^{n-1}b_n$.
- The Ratio Test states that if the limit of the ratio of consecutive terms a_{n+1}/a_n is less than 1, then the series is convergent. If the ratio is greater than 1, the series is divergent. If the limit is equal to 1, the test is inconclusive.
- The Root Test states that if $\lim_{n\to\infty} \sqrt[n]{|a_n|} < 1$, the series converges. If the same limit is greater than 1, the series diverges, and if the limit equals 1, the test is inconclusive.

Practice Questions

1. What is the solution to $4 \times 7 + (25 - 21)^2 \div 2$?

a. 512
b. 36
c. 60.5
d. 22
e. 16

2. Johnny earns $2334.50 from his job each month. He pays $1437 for monthly expenses. Johnny is planning a vacation in 3 months' time that he estimates will cost $1750 total. How much will Johnny have left over from three months' of saving once he pays for his vacation?

a. $948.50
b. $584.50
c. $852.50
d. $942.50
e. $848.50

3. What is the solution to $(2 \times 20) \div (7 + 1) + (6 \times 0.01) + (4 \times 0.001)$?

a. 5.064
b. 5.64
c. 5.0064
d. 48.064
e. 56.4

4. A piggy bank contains 12 dollars' worth of nickels. A nickel weighs 5 grams, and the empty piggy bank weighs 1050 grams. What is the total weight of the full piggy bank?

a. 1,110 grams
b. 1,200 grams
c. 2,110 grams
d. 2,200 grams
e. 2,250 grams

5. Last year, the New York City area received approximately $27\,{}^{3}/_{4}$ inches of snow. The Denver area received approximately 3 times as much snow as New York City. How much snow fell in Denver?

a. 60 inches
b. $27\,{}^{1}/_{4}$ inches
c. $9\,{}^{1}/_{4}$ inches
d. $83\,{}^{1}/_{4}$ inches
e. $29\,{}^{1}/_{4}$ inches

6. What is the product of two irrational numbers?

a. Irrational
b. Rational
c. Irrational or rational
d. Complex and imaginary
e. Imaginary

7. Which of the following augmented matrices represents the system of equations below?

$$2x - 3y + z = -5$$
$$4x - y - 2z = -7$$
$$-x + 2z = -1$$

a. $\begin{bmatrix} 2 & -3 & 1 & 5 \\ 4 & -1 & 0 & -7 \\ -1 & 0 & 2 & 1 \end{bmatrix}$

b. $\begin{bmatrix} 2 & 4 & -1 \\ -3 & -1 & 0 \\ 1 & -2 & 2 \\ -5 & -7 & -1 \end{bmatrix}$

c. $\begin{bmatrix} 2 & 4 & -1 & -5 \\ -3 & -1 & 0 & -7 \\ 2 & -2 & 2 & -1 \end{bmatrix}$

d. $\begin{bmatrix} 2 & -3 & 1 \\ 4 & -1 & -2 \\ -1 & 0 & 2 \end{bmatrix}$

e. $\begin{bmatrix} 2 & -3 & 1 & -5 \\ 4 & -1 & -2 & -7 \\ -1 & 0 & 2 & -1 \end{bmatrix}$

8. Which of the following correctly arranges the numbers from least to greatest value?

$0.85, \frac{4}{5}, \frac{2}{3}, \frac{91}{100}$

a. $0.85, \frac{4}{5}, \frac{2}{3}, \frac{91}{100}$

b. $\frac{4}{5}, 0.85, \frac{91}{100}, \frac{2}{3}$

c. $\frac{2}{3}, \frac{4}{5}, 0.85, \frac{91}{100}$

d. $0.85, \frac{91}{100}, \frac{4}{5}, \frac{2}{3}$

e. $\frac{4}{5}, \frac{2}{3}, 0.85, \frac{91}{100}$

9. Four people split a bill. The first person pays for $\frac{1}{5}$, the second person pays for $\frac{1}{4}$, and the third person pays for $\frac{1}{3}$. What fraction of the bill does the fourth person pay?

a. $\frac{1}{12}$

b. $\frac{47}{60}$

c. $\frac{1}{4}$

d. $\frac{4}{15}$

e. $\frac{13}{60}$

10. In a school with 300 students, there are 10 students with red hair, 50 students with black hair, 180 students with brown hair, and 60 students with blonde hair. What is the ratio of blonde hair to brown hair?

a. 3:1
b. 2:1
c. 1:3
d. 1:2
e. 1:5

Answer Explanations

1. B: To solve this correctly, keep in mind the order of operations with the mnemonic PEMDAS (Please Excuse My Dear Aunt Sally). This stands for Parentheses, Exponents, Multiplication, Division, Addition, Subtraction. Taking it step by step, solve the parentheses first:

$4 \text{ x } 7 + (4)^2 \div 2$

Then, apply the exponent:

$4 \text{ x } 7 + 16 \div 2$

Multiplication and division are both performed next:

$28 + 8 = 36$

2. D: First, subtract \$1437 from \$2334.50 to find Johnny's monthly savings; this equals \$897.50. Then, multiply this amount by 3 to find out how much he will have (in three months) before he pays for his vacation: this equals \$2692.50. Finally, subtract the cost of the vacation (\$1750) from this amount to find how much Johnny will have left: \$942.50.

3. A: Operations within the parentheses must be completed first. Then, division is completed. Finally, addition is the last operation to complete. When adding decimals, digits within each place value are added together. Therefore, the expression is evaluated as $(2 \times 20) \div (7 + 1) + (6 \times 0.01) + (4 \times 0.001) = 40 \div 8 + 0.06 + 0.004 = 5 + 0.06 + 0.004 = 5.064$.

4. E: A dollar contains 20 nickels. Therefore, if there are 12 dollars' worth of nickels, there are $12 \times 20 = 240$ nickels. Each nickel weighs 5 grams. Therefore, the weight of the nickels is $240 \times 5 = 1{,}200$ grams. Adding in the weight of the empty piggy bank, the filled bank weighs 2,250 grams.

5. D: 3 must be multiplied times $27\,{}^{3}/_{4}$. In order to easily do this, the mixed number should be converted into an improper fraction. $27\,{}^{3}/_{4} = {}^{27 * 4 + 3}/_{4} = {}^{111}/_{4}$. Therefore, Denver had approximately $3 \times {}^{111}/_{4} = {}^{333}/_{4}$ inches of snow. The improper fraction can be converted back into a mixed number through division. ${}^{333}/_{4} = 83\,{}^{1}/_{4}$ inches.

6. C: The product of two irrational numbers can be rational or irrational. Sometimes, the irrational parts of the two numbers cancel each other out, leaving a rational number. For example, $\sqrt{2} * \sqrt{2} = 2$ because the roots cancel each other out. Technically, the product of two irrational numbers can be complex because complex numbers can have either the real or imaginary part (in this case, the imaginary part) equal zero and still be considered a complex number. However, Choice *D* is incorrect because the product of two irrational numbers is not an imaginary number so saying the product is complex *and* imaginary is incorrect.

7. E: The augmented matrix that represents the system of equations has dimensions 4 x 3 because there are three equations with three unknowns. The coefficients of the variables make up the first three columns, and the last column is made up of the numbers to the right of the equals sign. This system can be solved by reducing the matrix to row-echelon form, where the last column gives the solution for the unknown variables.

8. C: The first step is to depict each number using decimals. $\frac{91}{100}$ = 0.91

Multiplying both the numerator and denominator of $\frac{4}{5}$ by 20 makes it $\frac{80}{100}$ or 0.80; the closest approximation of $\frac{2}{3}$ would be $\frac{66}{100}$ or 0.66 recurring. Rearrange each expression in ascending order, as found in answer *C*.

9. E: To find the fraction of the bill that the first three people pay, the fractions need to be added, which means finding common denominator. The common denominator will be 60.

$$\frac{1}{5}+\frac{1}{4}+\frac{1}{3}=\frac{12}{60}+\frac{15}{60}+\frac{20}{60}=\frac{47}{60}$$

The remainder of the bill is $1-\frac{47}{60}=\frac{60}{60}-\frac{47}{60}=\frac{13}{60}$.

10. C: There are 60 students with blonde hair and 180 students with brown hair. The ratio would be set up as blonde:brown, so 60:180. When reduced this is 1:3. This means that for every 1 student with blonde hair, there are 3 with brown hair.

Algebra and Functions

Relations and Functions

First, it's important to understand the definition of a *relation*. Given two variables, *x* and *y*, which stand for unknown numbers, a *relation* between *x* and *y* is an object that splits all of the pairs (*x*, *y*) into those for which the relation is true and those for which it is false. For example, consider the relation of $x^2 = y^2$. This relationship is true for the pair (1, 1) and for the pair (-2, 2), but false for (2, 3). Another example of a relation is $x \leq y$. This is true whenever *x* is less than or equal to *y*.

A *function* is a special kind of relation where, for each value of *x*, there is only a single value of *y* that satisfies the relation. So, $x^2 = y^2$ is *not* a function because in this case, if *x* is 1, *y* can be either 1 or -1: the pair (1, 1) and (1, -1) both satisfy the relation. More generally, for this relation, any pair of the form $(a, \pm a)$ will satisfy it. On the other hand, consider the following relation: $y = x^2 + 1$. This is a function because for each value of *x*, there is a unique value of *y* that satisfies the relation. Notice, however, there are multiple values of *x* that give us the same value of *y*. This is perfectly acceptable for a function. Therefore, *y* is a function of *x*.

To determine if a relation is a function, check to see if every *x* value has a unique corresponding *y* value.

A function can be viewed as an object that has *x* as its input and outputs a unique *y*-value. It is sometimes convenient to express this using *function notation*, where the function itself is given a name, often *f*. To emphasize that *f* takes *x* as its input, the function is written as $f(x)$. In the above example, the equation could be rewritten as $f(x) = x^2 + 1$. To write the value that a function yields for some specific value of *x*, that value is put in place of *x* in the function notation. For example, $f(3)$ means the value that the function outputs when the input value is 3. If $f(x) = x^2 + 1$, then $f(3) = 3^2 + 1 = 10$.

A function can also be viewed as a table of pairs (*x*, *y*), which lists the value for *y* for each possible value of *x*.

The set of all possible values for *x* in $f(x)$ is called the *domain* of the function, and the set of all possible outputs is called the *range* of the function. Note that usually the domain is assumed to be all real numbers, except those for which the expression for $f(x)$ is not defined, unless the problem specifies otherwise. An example of how a function might not be defined is in the case of $f(x) = \frac{1}{x+1}$, which is not defined when $x = -1$ (which would require dividing by zero). Therefore, in this case the domain would be all real numbers except $x = -1$.

If *y* is a function of *x*, then *x* is the *independent variable* and *y* is the *dependent variable*. This is because in many cases, the problem will start with some value of *x* and then see how *y* changes depending on this starting value.

Evaluating Functions

To evaluate functions, plug in the given value everywhere the variable appears in the expression for the function. For example, find $g(-2)$ where $g(x) = 2x^2 - \frac{4}{x}$. To complete the problem, plug in -2 in the following way:

$$g(-2) = 2(-2)^2 - \frac{4}{-2} = 2 \cdot 4 + 2 = 8 + 2 = 10$$

Defining Linear Equations

A function is called *linear* if it can take the form of the equation $f(x) = ax + b$, or $y = ax + b$, for any two numbers *a* and *b*. A linear equation forms a straight line when graphed on the coordinate plane. An example of a linear function is shown below on the graph.

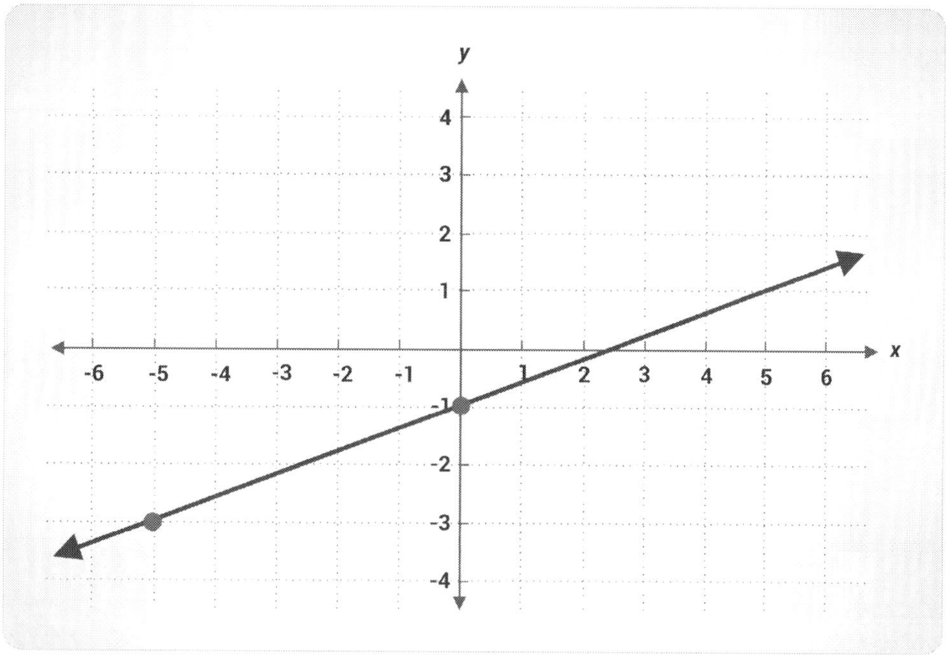

This is a graph of the following function: $y = \frac{2}{5}x - 1$. A table of values that satisfies this function is shown below.

x	y
-5	-3
0	-1
5	1
10	3

These points can be found on the graph using the form (x,y). For more on graphing in the coordinate plane, refer to the Graphing section below.

Forms of Linear Equations

When graphing a linear function, note that the ratio of the change of the *y* coordinate to the change in the *x* coordinate is constant between any two points on the resulting line, no matter which two points are chosen. In other words, in a pair of points on a line, (x_1, y_1) and (x_2, y_2), with $x_1 \neq x_2$ so that the two points are distinct, then the ratio $\frac{y_2 - y_1}{x_2 - x_1}$ will be the same, regardless of which particular pair of points are chosen. This ratio, $\frac{y_2-y_1}{x_2-x_1}$, is called the *slope* of the line and is frequently denoted with the letter m. If slope m is positive, then the line goes upward when moving to the right, while if slope m is negative, then the line goes downward when moving to the right. If the slope is 0, then the line is called *horizontal*, and the *y* coordinate is constant along the entire line. In lines where the *x* coordinate is constant along the entire line, *y* is not actually a function of *x*. For such lines, the slope is not defined. These lines are called *vertical* lines.

Linear functions may take forms other than $y = ax + b$. The most common forms of linear equations are explained below:

1. Standard Form: $Ax + By = C$, in which the slope is given by $m = \frac{-A}{B}$, and the *y*-intercept is given by $\frac{C}{B}$.

2. Slope-Intercept Form: $y = mx + b$, where the slope is *m* and the *y* intercept is *b*.

3. Point-Slope Form: $y - y_1 = m(x - x_1)$, where the slope is *m* and (x_1, y_1) is any point on the chosen line.

4. Two-Point Form: $\frac{y-y_1}{x-x_1} = \frac{y_2-y_1}{x_2-x_1}$, where (x_1, y_1) and (x_2, y_2) are any two distinct points on the chosen line. Note that the slope is given by $m = \frac{y_2-y_1}{x_2-x_1}$.

5. Intercept Form: $\frac{x}{x_1} + \frac{y}{y_1} = 1$, in which x_1 is the *x*-intercept and y_1 is the *y*-intercept.

These five ways to write linear equations are all useful in different circumstances. Depending on the given information, it may be easier to write one of the forms over another.

If $y = mx$, *y* is directly proportional to *x*. In this case, changing *x* by a factor changes *y* by that same factor. If $y = \frac{m}{x}$, *y* is inversely proportional to *x*. For example, if *x* is increased by a factor of 3, then *y* will be decreased by the same factor, 3.

Creating, Solving, or Interpreting a Linear Expression or Equation in One Variable

Linear expressions and equations are concise mathematical statements that can be written to model a variety of scenarios. Questions found pertaining to this topic will contain one variable only. A variable is an unknown quantity, usually denoted by a letter (*x, n, p,* etc.). In the case of linear expressions and equations, the power of the variable (its exponent) is 1. A variable without a visible exponent is raised to the first power.

<u>Writing Linear Expressions and Equations</u>
A linear expression is a statement about an unknown quantity expressed in mathematical symbols. The statement "five times a number added to forty" can be expressed as $5x + 40$. A linear equation is a statement in which two expressions (at least one containing a variable) are equal to each other. The statement "five times a number added to forty is equal to ten" can be expressed as $5x + 40 = 10$. Real-world scenarios can also be expressed mathematically. Consider the following:

> Bob had $20 and Tom had $4. After selling 4 ice cream cones to Bob, Tom has as much money as Bob.

The cost of an ice cream cone is an unknown quantity and can be represented by a variable. The amount of money Bob has after his purchase is four times the cost of an ice cream cone subtracted from his original \$20. The amount of money Tom has after his sale is four times the cost of an ice cream cone added to his original \$4. This can be expressed as: $20 - 4x = 4x + 4$, where *x* represents the cost of an ice cream cone.

When expressing a verbal or written statement mathematically, it is key to understand words or phrases that can be represented with symbols. The following are examples:

Symbol	**Phrase**
$+$	added to, increased by, sum of, more than
$-$	decreased by, difference between, less than, take away
x	multiplied by, 3 (4, 5 . . .) times as large, product of
$\div$	divided by, quotient of, half (third, etc.) of
$=$	is, the same as, results in, as much as
$x, t, n, etc.$	a number, unknown quantity, value of

Evaluating and Simplifying Algebraic Expressions

Given an algebraic expression, students may be asked to evaluate for given values of variable(s). In doing so, students will arrive at a numerical value as an answer. For example:

Evaluate $a - 2b + ab\ for\ a = 3 \text{ and } b = -1$

To evaluate an expression, the given values should be substituted for the variables and simplified using the order of operations. In this case: $(3) - 2(-1) + (3)(-1)$. Parentheses are used when substituting.

Given an algebraic expression, students may be asked to simplify the expression. For example:

Simplify $5x^2 - 10x + 2 - 8x^2 + x - 1$.

Simplifying algebraic expressions requires combining like terms. A term is a number, variable, or product of a number and variables separated by addition and subtraction. The terms in the above expressions are: $5x^2, -10x, 2, -8x^2, x$, and -1. Like terms have the same variables raised to the same powers (exponents). To combine like terms, the coefficients (numerical factor of the term including sign) are added, while the variables and their powers are kept the same. The example above simplifies to $-3x^2 - 9x + 1$.

Solving Linear Equations

When asked to solve a linear equation, it requires determining a numerical value for the unknown variable. Given a linear equation involving addition, subtraction, multiplication, and division, isolation of the variable is done by working backward. Addition and subtraction are inverse operations, as are multiplication and division; therefore, they can be used to cancel each other out.

The first steps to solving linear equations are to distribute if necessary and combine any like terms that are on the same side of the equation. Sides of an equation are separated by an $=$ sign. Next, the equation should be manipulated to get the variable on one side. Whatever is done to one side of an equation, must be done to the other side to remain equal. Then, the variable should be isolated by using inverse operations to undo the order of operations backward. Undo addition and subtraction, then undo multiplication and division. For example:

Solve $4(t-2)+2t-4=2(9-2t)$

Distribute: $4t-8+2t-4=18-4t$

Combine like terms: $6t-12=18-4t$

Add 4t to each side to move the variable: $10t-12=18$

Add 12 to each side to isolate the variable: $10t=30$

Divide each side by 10 to isolate the variable: $t=3$

The answer can be checked by substituting the value for the variable into the original equation and ensuring both sides calculate to be equal.

Creating, Solving, or Interpreting Linear Inequalities in One Variable

Linear inequalities and linear equations are both comparisons of two algebraic expressions. However, unlike equations in which the expressions are equal to each other, linear inequalities compare expressions that are unequal. Linear equations typically have one value for the variable that makes the statement true. Linear inequalities generally have an infinite number of values that make the statement true. Exceptions to these last two statements are covered in Section 6.

Writing Linear Inequalities

Linear inequalities are a concise mathematical way to express the relationship between unequal values. More specifically, they describe in what way the values are unequal. A value could be greater than (>); less than (<); greater than or equal to (≥); or less than or equal to (≤) another value. The statement "five times a number added to forty is more than sixty-five" can be expressed as $5x+40>65$. Common words and phrases that express inequalities are:

Symbol	**Phrase**
$<$	is under, is below, smaller than, beneath
$>$	is above, is over, bigger than, exceeds
$\leq$	no more than, at most, maximum
$\geq$	no less than, at least, minimum

Solving Linear Inequalities

When solving a linear inequality, the solution is the set of all numbers that makes the statement true. The inequality $x+2\geq 6$ has a solution set of 4 and every number greater than 4 (4.0001, 5, 12, 107, etc.). Adding 2 to 4 or any number greater than 4 would result in a value that is greater than or equal to 6. Therefore, $x\geq 4$ would be the solution set.

Solution sets for linear inequalities often will be displayed using a number line. If a value is included in the set (≥ or ≤), there is a shaded dot placed on that value and an arrow extending in the direction of the solutions. For a variable $>$ or $\geq$ a number, the arrow would point right on the number line (the direction where the numbers increase); and if a variable is $<$ or $\leq$ a number, the arrow would point left (where the numbers decrease). If the value is not included in the set ($>$ or $<$), an open circle on that value would be used with an arrow in the appropriate direction.

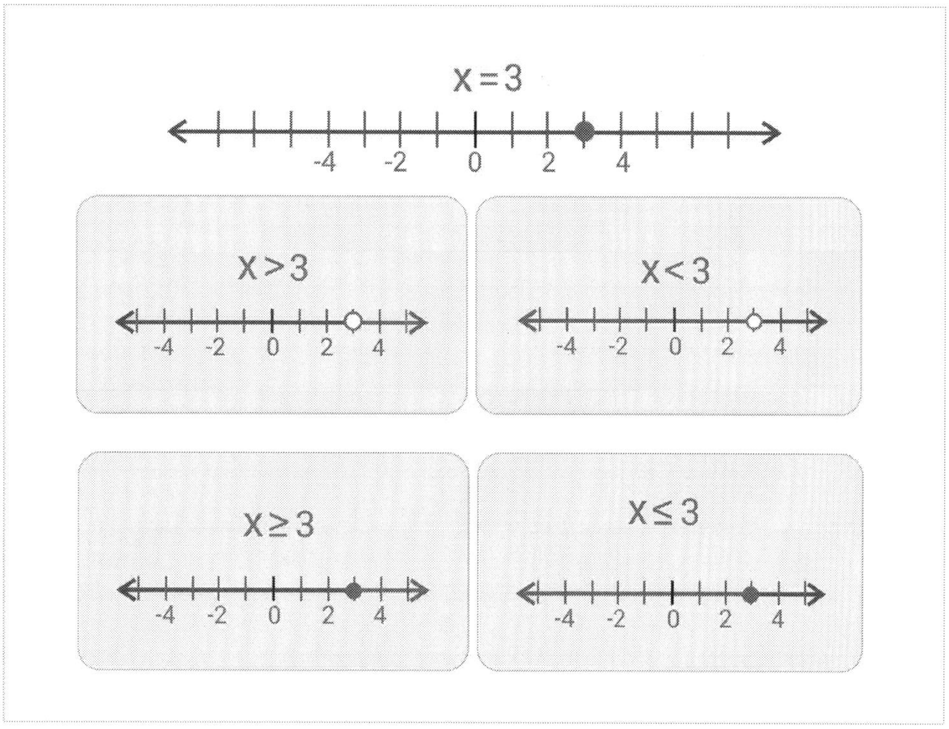

Students may be asked to write a linear inequality given a graph of its solution set. To do so, they should identify whether the value is included (shaded dot or open circle) and the direction in which the arrow is pointing.

In order to algebraically solve a linear inequality, the same steps should be followed as in solving a linear equation (see section on *Solving Linear Equations*). The inequality symbol stays the same for all operations EXCEPT when dividing by a negative number. If dividing by a negative number while solving an inequality, the relationship reverses (the sign flips). Dividing by a positive does not change the relationship, so the sign stays the same. In other words, $>$ switches to $<$ and vice versa. An example is shown below.

Solve $-2(x+4) \leq 22$

Distribute: $-2x - 8 \leq 22$

Add 8 to both sides: $-2x \leq 30$

Divide both sides by -2: $x \geq 15$

Building a Linear Function that Models a Linear Relationship Between Two Quantities

Linear relationships between two quantities can be expressed in two ways: function notation or as a linear equation with two variables. The relationship is referred to as linear because its graph is represented by a line. For a relationship to be linear, both variables must be raised to the first power only.

Function/Linear Equation Notation

A relation is a set of input and output values that can be written as ordered pairs. A function is a relation in which each input is paired with exactly one output. The domain of a function consists of all inputs, and the range consists of all outputs. Graphing the ordered pairs of a linear function produces a straight line. An example of a function would be $f(x) = 4x + 4$, read "*f* of *x* is equal to four times *x* plus four." In this example, the input would be *x* and the output would be f(*x*). Ordered pairs would be represented as (*x*, f(*x*)). To find the output for an input value of 3, 3 would be substituted for *x* into the function as follows: $f(3) = 4(3) + 4$, resulting in $f(3) = 16$. Therefore, the ordered pair $(3, f(3)) = (3, 16)$. Note f(*x*) is a function of *x* denoted by *f*. Functions of *x* could be named *g*(*x*), read "*g* of *x*"; *p*(*x*), read "*p* of *x*"; etc.

A linear function could also be written in the form of an equation with two variables. Typically, the variable *x* represents the inputs and the variable *y* represents the outputs. The variable *x* is considered the independent variable and *y* the dependent variable. The above function would be written as $y = 4x + 4$. Ordered pairs are written in the form (*x*, *y*).

Writing Linear Equations in Two Variables

When writing linear equations in two variables, the process depends on the information given. Questions will typically provide the slope of the line and its *y*-intercept, an ordered pair and the slope, or two ordered pairs.

Given the Slope and Y-Intercept

Linear equations are commonly written in slope-intercept form, $y = mx + b$, where *m* represents the slope of the line and *b* represents the *y*-intercept. The slope is the rate of change between the variables, usually expressed as a whole number or fraction. The *y*-intercept is the value of *y* when *x* = 0 (the point where the line intercepts the *y*-axis on a graph). Given the slope and *y*-intercept of a line, the values are substituted for *m* and *b* into the equation. A line with a slope of ½ and *y*-intercept of -2 would have an equation $y = \frac{1}{2}x - 2$.

Given an Ordered Pair and the Slope

The point-slope form of a line, $y - y_1 = m(x - x_1)$, is used to write an equation when given an ordered pair (point on the equation's graph) for the function and its rate of change (slope of the line). The values for the slope, *m*, and the point (x_1, y_1) are substituted into the point-slope form to obtain the equation of the line. A line with a slope of 3 and an ordered pair (4, -2) would have an equation $y - (-2) = 3(x - 4)$. If a question specifies that the equation be written in slope-intercept form, the equation should be manipulated to isolate *y*:

Solve: $y - (-2) = 3(x - 4)$

Distribute: $y + 2 = 3x - 12$

Subtract 2 from both sides: $y = 3x - 14$

Given Two Ordered Pairs

Given two ordered pairs for a function, (x_1, y_1) and (x_2, y_2), it is possible to determine the rate of change between the variables (slope of the line). To calculate the slope of the line, m, the values for the ordered pairs should be substituted into the formula:

$$m = \frac{y_2 - y_1}{x_2 - x_1}$$

The expression is substituted to obtain a whole number or fraction for the slope. Once the slope is calculated, the slope and either of the ordered pairs should be substituted into the point-slope form to obtain the equation of the line.

Creating, Solving, and Interpreting Systems of Linear Inequalities in Two Variables

<u>Expressing Linear Inequalities in Two Variables</u>
A linear inequality in two variables is a statement expressing an unequal relationship between those two variables. Typically written in slope-intercept form, the variable *y* can be greater than; less than; greater than or equal to; or less than or equal to a linear expression including the variable *x*. Examples include $y > 3x$ and $y \leq ½x - 3$. Questions may instruct students to model real world scenarios such as:

> You work part-time cutting lawns for $15 each and cleaning houses for $25 each. Your goal is to make more than $90 this week. Write an inequality to represent the possible pairs of lawns and houses needed to reach your goal.

This scenario can be expressed as $15x + 25y > 90$ where *x* is the number of lawns cut and *y* is the number of houses cleaned.

<u>Graphing Solution Sets for Linear Inequalities in Two Variables</u>
A graph of the solution set for a linear inequality shows the ordered pairs that make the statement true. The graph consists of a boundary line dividing the coordinate plane and shading on one side of the boundary. The boundary line should be graphed just as a linear equation would be graphed (see section on *Understanding Connections Between Algebraic and Graphical Representations*). If the inequality symbol is $>$ or $<$, a dashed line can be used to indicate that the line is not part of the solution set. If the inequality symbol is $\geq$ or $\leq$, a solid line can be used to indicate that the boundary line is included in the solution set. An ordered pair (*x*, *y*) on either side of the line should be chosen to test in the inequality statement. If substituting the values for *x* and *y* results in a true statement ($15(3) + 25(2) > 90$), that ordered pair and all others on that side of the boundary line are part of the solution set. To indicate this, that region of the graph should be shaded. If substituting the ordered pair results in a false statement, the ordered pair and all others on that side are not part of the solution set.

Therefore, the other region of the graph contains the solutions and should be shaded.

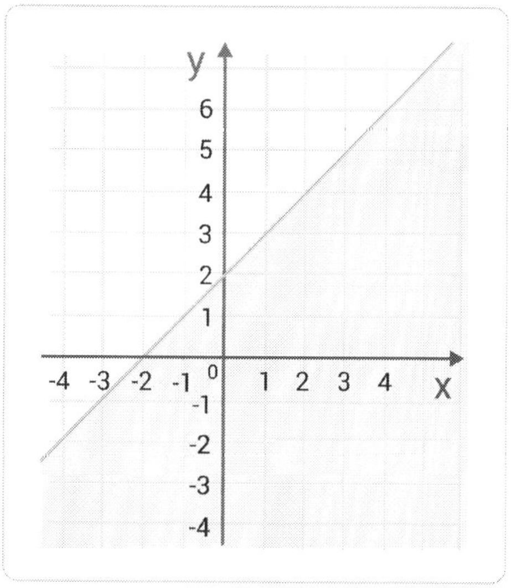

A question may simply ask whether a given ordered pair is a solution to a given inequality. To determine this, the values should be substituted for the ordered pair into the inequality. If the result is a true statement, the ordered pair is a solution; if the result is a false statement, the ordered pair is not a solution.

Expressing Systems of Linear Inequalities in Two Variables

A system of linear inequalities consists of two linear inequalities making comparisons between two variables. Students may be given a scenario and asked to express it as a system of inequalities:

> A consumer study calls for at least 60 adult participants. It cannot use more than 25 men. Express these constraints as a system of inequalities.

This can be modeled by the system: $x + y \geq 60; x \leq 25$, where *x* represents the number of men and *y* represents the number of women. A solution to the system is an ordered pair that makes both inequalities true when substituting the values for *x* and *y*.

Graphing Solution Sets for Systems of Linear Inequalities in Two Variables

The solution set for a system of inequalities is the region of a graph consisting of ordered pairs that make both inequalities true. To graph the solution set, each linear inequality should first be graphed with appropriate shading. The region of the graph should be identified where the shading for the two inequalities overlaps. This region contains the solution set for the system.

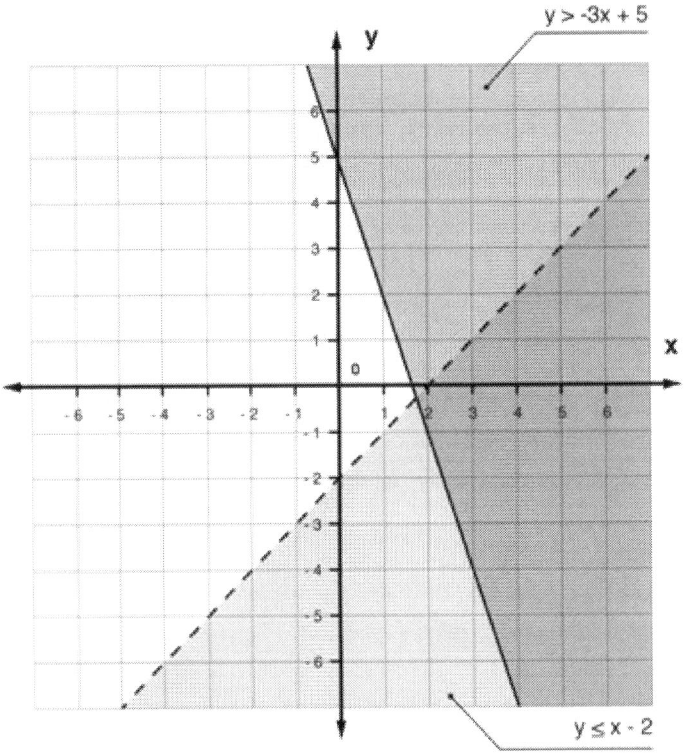

An ordered pair from the region of solutions can be selected to test in the system of inequalities.

Just as with manipulating linear inequalities in one variable, if dividing by a negative number in working with a linear inequality in two variables, the relationship reverses and the inequality sign should be flipped.

Creating, Solving, and Interpreting Systems of Two Linear Equations in Two Variables

Expressing Systems of Two Linear Equations in Two Variables

A system of two linear equations in two variables is a set of equations that use the same variables, usually *x* and *y*. Here's a sample problem:

> An Internet provider charges an installation fee and a monthly charge. It advertises that two months of its offering costs $100 and six months costs $200. Find the monthly charge and the installation fee.

The two unknown quantities (variables) are the monthly charge and the installation fee. There are two different statements given relating the variables: two months added to the installation fee is $100; and six months added to the installation fee is $200. Using the variable *x* as the monthly charge and *y* as the installation fee, the statements can be written as the following: $2x + y = 100$; $6x + y = 200$. These two equations taken together form a system modeling the given scenario.

Solutions of a System of Two Linear Equations in Two Variables

A solution for a system of equations is an ordered pair that makes both equations true. One method for solving a system of equations is to graph both lines on a coordinate plane (see section on *Understanding Connections Between Algebraic and Graphical Representations*). If the lines intersect, the point of intersection is the solution to the system. Every point on a line represents an ordered pair that makes its equation true. The ordered pair represented by this point of intersection lies on both lines and therefore makes both equations true. This ordered pair should be checked by substituting its values into both of the original equations of the system. Note that given a system of equations and an ordered pair, the ordered pair can be determined to be a solution or not by checking it in both equations.

If, when graphed, the lines representing the equations of a system do not intersect, then the two lines are parallel to each other or they are the same exact line. Parallel lines extend in the same direction without ever meeting. A system consisting of parallel lines has no solution. If the equations for a system represent the same exact line, then every point on the line is a solution to the system. In this case, there would be an infinite number of solutions. A system consisting of intersecting lines is referred to as independent; a system consisting of parallel lines is referred to as inconsistent; and a system consisting of coinciding lines is referred to as dependent.

Parallel Lines	**Intersecting Lines**	**Coincident Lines**
Inconsistent	Independent	Dependent

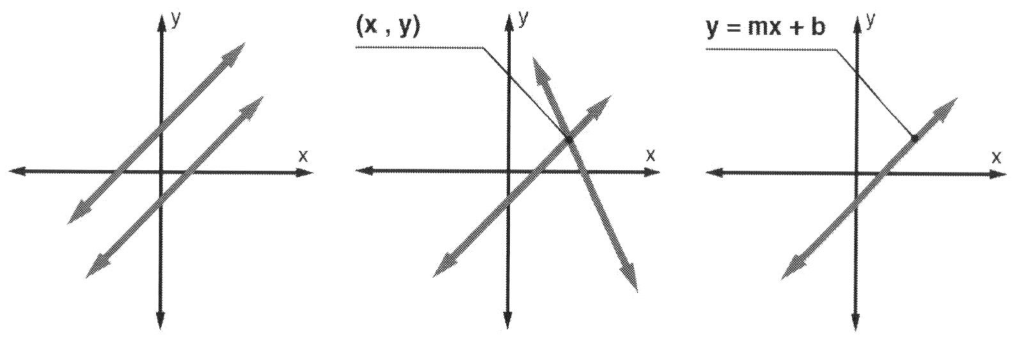

Algebraically Solving Linear Equations (or Inequalities) in One Variable

Linear equations in one variable and linear inequalities in one variable can be solved following similar processes. Although they typically have one solution, a linear equation can have no solution or can have a solution set of all real numbers. Solution sets for linear inequalities typically consist of an infinite number of values either greater or less than a given value (where the given value may or may not be included in the set). However, a linear inequality can have no solution or can have a solution set consisting of all real numbers.

Linear Equations in One Variable – Special Cases

Solving a linear equation produces a value for the variable that makes the algebraic statement true. If there is no value for the variable that would make the statement true, there is no solution to the equation. Here's a sample equation: $x + 3 = x - 1$. There is no value for *x* in which adding 3 to the value would produce the same result as subtracting 1 from that value. Conversely, if any value for the variable would make a true statement, the equation has an infinite number of solutions. Here's another sample equation: $3x + 6 = 3(x + 2)$. Any real number substituted for *x* would result in a true statement (both sides of the equation are equal).

By manipulating equations similar to the two above, the variable of the equation will cancel out completely. If the constants that are left express a true statement (ex., $6 = 6$), then all real numbers are solutions to the equation. If the constants left express a false statement (ex., $3 = -1$), then there is no solution to the equation.

A question on this material may present a linear equation with an unknown value for either a constant or a coefficient of the variable and ask to determine the value that produces an equation with no solution or infinite solutions. For example:

> $3x + 7 = 3x + 10 + n$; Find the value of *n* that would create an equation with an infinite number of solutions for the variable *x*.

To solve this problem, the equation should be manipulated so the variable *x* will cancel. To do this, 3*x* should be subtracted from both sides, which would leave $7 = 10 + n$. By subtracting 10 on both sides, it is determined that $n = -3$. Therefore, a value of -3 for *n* would result in an equation with a solution set of all real numbers.

If the same problem asked for the equation to have no solution, the value of *n* would be all real numbers except -3.

Linear Inequalities in One Variable – Special Cases

A linear inequality can have a solution set consisting of all real numbers or can contain no solution. When solved algebraically, a linear inequality in which the variable cancels out and results in a true statement (ex., $7 \geq 2$) has a solution set of all real numbers. A linear inequality in which the variable cancels out and results in a false statement (ex., $7 \leq 2$) has no solution.

Compound Inequalities

A compound inequality is a pair of inequalities joined by *and* or *or*. Given a compound inequality, to determine its solution set, both inequalities should be solved for the given variable. The solution set for a compound inequality containing *and* consists of all the values for the variable that make both inequalities true. If solving the compound inequality results in $x > -9$ and $x \leq 6$, the solution set would consist of all values between -2 and 3, including 3. This may also be written as follows: $-9 < x \leq 6$. Due to the graphs of their solution sets (shown below), compound inequalities such as these are referred to as conjunctions.

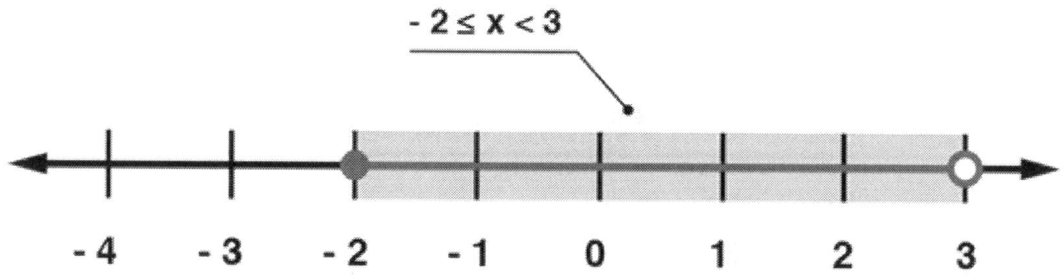

If there are no values that would make both inequalities of a compound inequality containing *and* true, then there is no solution. An example would be $x > 2$ and $x \leq 0$.

The solution set for a compound inequality containing *or* consists of all the values for the variable that make at least one of the inequalities true. The solution set for the compound inequality $x \leq -2$ or $x > 1$ consists of all values less than 2, 6, and all values greater than 6. Due to the graphs of their solution sets (shown below), compound inequalities such as these are referred to as disjunctions.

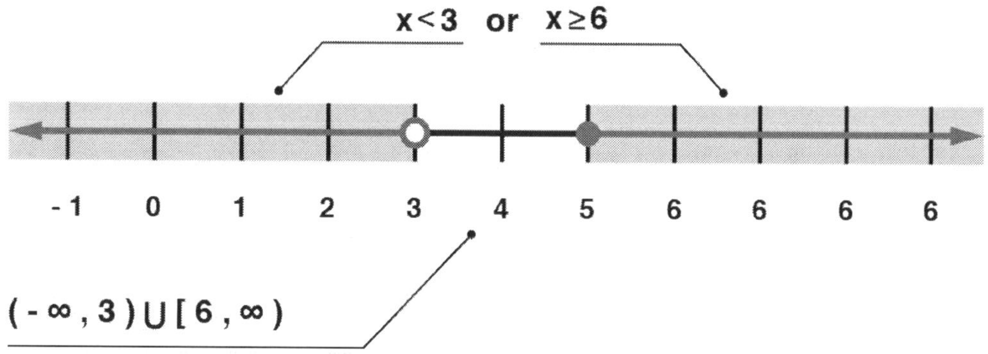

If the two inequalities for a compound inequality containing *or* "overlap," then the solution set contains all real numbers. An example would be $x > 2$ or $x < 7$. Any number would make at least one of these true.

Algebraically Solving Systems of Two Linear Equations in Two Variables

A system of two linear equations in two variables is a set of equations that use the same variables (typically *x* and *y*). A solution to the system is an ordered pair that makes both equations true. One method for solving a system is by graphing as explained in Section 5.2. This method, however, is not always practical. Students may not have graph paper; or the solution may not consist of integers, making it difficult to identify the exact point of intersection on a graph. There are two methods for solving systems of equations algebraically: substitution and elimination. The method used will depend on the characteristics of the equations in the system.

Solving Systems of Equations with the Substitution Method
If one of the equations in a system has an isolated variable (*x*= or *y*=) or a variable that can be easily isolated, the substitution method can be used. Here's a sample system: $x + 3y = 7; 2x - 4y = 24$. The first equation can easily be solved for *x*. By subtracting 3*y* on both sides, the resulting equation is $x =$

$7 - 3y$. When one equation is solved for a variable, the expression that it is equal can be substituted into the other equation. For this example, $(7 - 3y)$ would be substituted for *x* into the second equation as follows: $2(7 - 3y) + 4y = 24$. Solving this equation results in $y = -5$. Once the value for one variable is known, this value should be substituted into either of the original equations to determine the value of the other variable. For the example, -5 would be substituted for *y* in either of the original equations. Substituting into the first equation results in $x + 3(-5) = 7$, and solving this equation yields $x = 22$. The solution to a system is an ordered pair, so the solution to the example is written as (22, 7). The solution can be checked by substituting it into both equations of the system to ensure it results in two true statements.

Solving Systems of Equations with the Elimination Method

The elimination method for solving a system of equations involves canceling out (or eliminating) one of the variables. This method is typically used when both equations of a system are written in standard form $(Ax + By = C)$. An example is $2x + 3y = 12; 5x - y = 13$. To perform the elimination method, the equations in the system should be arranged vertically to be added together and then one or both of the equations should be multiplied so that one variable will be eliminated when the two are added. Opposites will cancel each other when added together. For example, 8*x* and -8*x* will cancel each other when added. For the example above, writing the system vertically helps identify that the bottom equation should be multiplied by 3 to eliminate the variable *y*.

$$2x + 3y = 12 \quad \rightarrow \quad 2x + 3y = 12$$

$$3(5x - y = 13) \quad \rightarrow \quad 15x - 3y = 39$$

Adding the two equations together vertically results in $17x = 51$. Solving yields $x = 3$. Once the value for one variable is known, it can be substituted into either of the original equations to determine the value of the other variable. Once this is obtained, the solution can be written as an ordered pair (*x*, *y*) and checked in both equations of the system. In this example, the solution is (3, 2).

Systems of Equations with No Solution or an Infinite Number of Solutions

A system of equations can have one solution, no solution, or an infinite number of solutions. If, while solving a system algebraically, both variables cancel out, then the system has either no solution or has an infinite number of solutions. If the remaining constants result in a true statement (ex., $7 = 7$), then there is an infinite number of solutions. This would indicate coinciding lines. If the remaining constants result in a false statement, then there is no solution to the system. This would indicate parallel lines.

Interpreting Variables and Constants in Expressions for Linear Functions in the Context Presented

Linear functions, also written as linear equations in two variables, can be written to model real-world scenarios. Questions on this material will provide information about a scenario and then request a linear equation to represent the scenario. The algebraic process for writing the equation will depend on the given information. The key to writing linear models is to decipher the information given to determine what it represents in the context of a linear equation (variables, slope, ordered pairs, etc.).

Identifying Variables for Linear Models

The first step to writing a linear model is to identify what the variables represent. A variable represents an unknown quantity, and in the case of a linear equation, a specific relationship exists between the two variables (usually *x* and *y*). Within a given scenario, the variables are the two quantities that are changing. The variable *x* is considered the independent variable and represents the inputs of a function. The variable *y* is considered the dependent variable and represents the outputs of a function. For example, if a scenario describes distance traveled and time traveled, distance would be represented by *y* and time represented by *x*. The distance traveled depends on the time spent traveling (time is independent). If a scenario describes the cost of a cab ride and the distance traveled, the cost would be represented by *y* and the distance represented by *x*. The cost of a cab ride depends on the distance traveled.

Identifying the Slope and Y-Intercept for Linear Models

The slope of the graph of a line represents the rate of change between the variables of an equation. In the context of a real-world scenario, the slope will tell the way in which the unknown quantities (variables) change with respect to each other. A scenario involving distance and time might state that someone is traveling at a rate of 45 miles per hour. The slope of the linear model would be 45. A scenario involving the cost of a cab ride and distance traveled might state that the person is charged $3 for each mile. The slope of the linear model would be 3.

The *y*-intercept of a linear function is the value of *y* when $x = 0$ (the point where the line intercepts the *y*-axis on the graph of the equation). It is sometimes helpful to think of this as a "starting point" for a linear function. Suppose for the scenario about the cab ride that the person is told that the cab company charges a flat fee of $5 plus $3 for each mile. Before traveling any distance ($x = 0$), the cost is $5. The *y*-intercept for the linear model would be 5.

Identifying Ordered Pairs for Linear Models

A linear equation with two variables can be written given a point (ordered pair) and the slope or given two points on a line. An ordered pair gives a set of corresponding values for the two variables (*x* and *y*). As an example, for a scenario involving distance and time, it is given that the person traveled 112.5 miles in 2 ½ hours. Knowing that *x* represents time and *y* represents distance, this information can be written as the ordered pair (2.5, 112.5).

Polynomials

An expression of the form ax^n, where *n* is a non-negative integer, is called a *monomial* because it contains one term. A sum of monomials is called a *polynomial*. For example, $-4x^3 + x$ is a polynomial, while $5x^7$ is a monomial. A function equal to a polynomial is called a *polynomial function*.

The monomials in a polynomial are also called the *terms* of the polynomial.

The constants that precede the variables are called *coefficients*.

The highest value of the exponent of *x* in a polynomial is called the *degree* of the polynomial. So, $-4x^3 + x$ has a degree of 3, while $-2x^5 + x^3 + 4x + 1$ has a degree of 5. When multiplying polynomials, the degree of the result will be the sum of the degrees of the two polynomials being multiplied.

To add polynomials, add the coefficients of like powers of *x*. For example,

$$(-2x^5 + x^3 + 4x + 1) + (-4x^3 + x)$$

$$-2x^5 + (1 - 4)x^3 + (4 + 1)x + 1$$

$$-2x^5 - 3x^3 + 5x + 1$$

Likewise, subtraction of polynomials is performed by subtracting coefficients of like powers of *x*. So,

$$(-2x^5 + x^3 + 4x + 1) - (-4x^3 + x)$$

$$-2x^5 + (1 + 4)x^3 + (4 - 1)x + 1$$

$$-2x^5 + 5x^3 + 3x + 1$$

To multiply two polynomials, multiply each term of the first polynomial by each term of the second polynomial and add the results. For example:

$$(4x^2 + x)(-x^3 + x)$$

$$4x^2(-x^3) + 4x^2(x) + x(-x^3) + x(x)$$

$$-4x^5 + 4x^3 - x^4 + x^2$$

n the case where each polynomial has two terms, like in this example, some students find it helpful to remember this as multiplying the First terms, then the Outer terms, then the Inner terms, and finally the Last terms, with the mnemonic FOIL. For longer polynomials, the multiplication process is the same, but there will be, of course, more terms, and there is no common mnemonic to remember each combination.

The process of *factoring* a polynomial means to write the polynomial as a product of other (generally simpler) polynomials. Here is an example: $x^2 - 4x + 3 = (x - 1)(x - 3)$. If a certain monomial divides every term of the polynomial, factor it out of each term, for example:

$$4x^3 + 16x^2 = 4x^2(x + 4).$$

$$x^2 + 2xy + y^2 = (x + y)^2 \text{ or } x^2 - 2xy + y^2 = (x - y)^2$$

$$x^2 - y^2 = (x + y)(x - y)$$

$$x^3 + y^3 = (x + y)(x^2 - xy + y^2)$$

$$x^3 - y^3 = (x - y)(x^2 + xy + y^2)$$

$$x^3 + 3x^2y + 3xy^2 + y^3 = (x + y)^3 \text{ and } x^3 - 3x^2y + 3xy^2 - y^3 = (x - y)^3$$

It sometimes can be necessary to rewrite the polynomial in some clever way before applying the above rules. Consider the problem of factoring $x^4 - 1$. This does not immediately look like any of the cases for which there are rules. However, it's possible to think of this polynomial as $x^4 - 1 = (x^2)^2 - (1^2)^2$, and now apply the third rule in the above list to simplify this:

$$(x^2)^2 - (1^2)^2 = (x^2 + 1^2)(x^2 - 1^2) = (x^2 + 1)(x^2 - 1)$$

Exponents and Roots

An *exponent* is written as a^b. In this expression, *a* is called the *base* and *b* is called the *exponent*. It is properly stated that *a* is raised to the *n*-th power. Therefore, in the expression 2^3, the exponent is 3, while the base is 2. Such an expression is called an *exponential expression*. Note that when the exponent is 2, it is called *squaring* the base, and when it is 3, it is called *cubing* the base.

When the exponent is a positive integer, this indicates the base is multiplied by itself the number of times written in the exponent. So, in the expression 2^3, multiply 2 by itself with 3 copies of 2: $2^3 = 2 \cdot 2 \cdot 2 = 8$. One thing to notice is that, for positive integers *n* and *m*, $a^n a^m = a^{n+m}$ is a rule. In order to make this rule be true for an integer of 0, $a^0 = 1$, so that $a^n a^0 = a^{n+0} = a^n$. And, in order to make this rule be true for negative exponents, $a^{-n} = \frac{1}{a^n}$.

Another rule for simplifying expressions with exponents is shown by the following equation: $(a^m)^n = a^{mn}$. This is true for fractional exponents as well. So, for a positive integer, define $a^{\frac{1}{n}}$ to be the number that, when raised to the *n*-th power, provides *a*. In other words, $(a^{\frac{1}{n}})^n = a$ is the desired equation. It should be noted that $a^{\frac{1}{n}}$ is the *n*-th root of *a*. This also can be written as $a^{\frac{1}{n}} = \sqrt[n]{a}$. The symbol on the right-hand side of this equation is called a *radical*. If the root is left out, assume that the 2nd root should be taken, also called the *square* root: $a^{\frac{1}{2}} = \sqrt[2]{a} = \sqrt{a}$. Additionally, $\sqrt[3]{a}$ is also called the *cube* root.

Note that when multiple roots exist, $a^{\frac{1}{n}}$ is defined to be the *positive* root. So, $4^{\frac{1}{2}} = 2$. Also note that negative numbers do not have even roots in the real numbers.

This also enables finding exponents for any rational number:

$$a^{\frac{m}{n}} = (a^{\frac{1}{n}})^m = (a^m)^{\frac{1}{n}}$$

In fact, the exponent can be any real number. In general, the following rules for exponents should be used for any numbers $a, b, m,$ and n.

- $a^1 = a$.
- $1^a = 1$.
- $a^0 = 1$.
- $a^m a^n = a^{m+n}$.
- $\frac{a^m}{a^n} = a^{m-n}$
- $(a^m)^n = a^{m \times n}$.
- $(ab)^m = a^m b^m$.
- $(\frac{a}{b})^m = \frac{a^m}{b^m}$.

As an example of applying these rules, consider the problem of simplifying the expression $(3x^2y)^3(2xy^4)$. Start by simplifying the left term using the sixth rule listed. Applying this rule yields the following expression: $27x^6y^3(2xy^4)$. The exponents can now be combined with base *x* and the exponents with base *y*. Multiply the coefficients to yield $54x^7y^7$.

Finding the Zeros of a Function

The zeros of a function are the points where its graph crosses the x-axis. At these points, $y = 0$. One way to find the zeros is to analyze the graph. If given the graph, the x-coordinates can be found where the line crosses the x-axis. Another way to find the zeros is to set $y = 0$ in the equation and solve for x. Depending on the type of equation, this could be done by using opposite operations, by factoring the equation, by completing the square, or by using the quadratic formula. If a graph does not cross the x-axis, then the function may have complex roots.

Solving Equations with Exponents and Roots

Here are some of the most important properties of exponents and roots: if *n* is an integer, and if $a^n = b^n$, then $a = b$ if *n* is odd; but $a = \pm b$ if *n* is even. Similarly, if the roots of two things are equal, $\sqrt[n]{a} = \sqrt[n]{b}$, then $a = b$. This means that when starting with a true equation, both sides of that equation can be raised to a given power to obtain another true equation. Beware that when an even-powered root is taken on both sides of the equation, a $\pm$ in the result. For example, given the equation $x^2 = 16$, take the square root of both sides to solve for x. This results in the answer $x = \pm 4$ because $(-4)^2 = 16$ and $(4)^2 = 16$.

Another property is that if $a^n = a^m$, then $n = m$. This is true for any real numbers *n* and *m*.

For solving the equation $\sqrt{x+2} - 1 = 3$, start by moving the -1 over to the right-hand side. This is performed by adding 1 to both sides, which yields $\sqrt{x+2} = 4$. Now, square both sides, but remember that by squaring both sides, the signs are irrelevant. This yields $x + 2 = 16$, which simplifies to give $x = 14$.

Now consider the problem $(x+1)^4 = 16$. To solve this, take the 4th root of both sides, which means an ambiguity in the sign will be introduced because it is an even root:

$$\sqrt[4]{(x+1)^4} = \pm\sqrt[4]{16}$$

The right-hand side is 2, since $2^4 = 16$. Therefore, $x + 1 = \pm 2$ or $x = -1 \pm 2$. Thus, the two possible solutions are $x = -3$ and $x = 1$.

Remember that when solving equations, the answer can be checked by plugging the solution back into the problem to make a true statement.

Rational Expressions

A rational expression is a fraction where the numerator and denominator are both polynomials. Some examples of rational expressions include the following: $\frac{4x^3y^5}{3z^4}$, $\frac{4x^3+3x}{x^2}$, and $\frac{x^2+7x+10}{x+2}$. Since these refer to expressions and not equations, they can be simplified but not solved. Using the rules in the previous Exponents and Roots sections, some rational expressions with monomials can be simplified. Other rational expressions such as the last example, $\frac{x^2+7x+1}{x+2}$, take more steps to be simplified. First, the polynomial on top can be factored from $x^2 + 7x + 10$ into $(x+5)(x+2)$. Then the common factors can be canceled and the expression can be simplified to $(x+5)$.

Consider this problem as an example of using rational expressions. Reggie wants to lay sod in his rectangular backyard. The length of the yard is given by the expression $4x + 2$ and the width is unknown. The area of the yard is $20x + 10$. Reggie needs to find the width of the yard. Knowing that the area of a rectangle is length multiplied by width, an expression can be written to find the width: $\frac{20x+10}{4x+2}$, area divided by length. Simplifying this expression by factoring out 10 on the top and 2 on the bottom leads to this expression: $\frac{10(2x+1)}{2(2x+1)}$. By cancelling out the $2x + 1$, that results in $\frac{10}{2} = 5$. The width of the yard is found to be 5 by simplifying a rational expression.

Rational Equations

A *rational equation* can be as simple as an equation with a ratio of polynomials, $\frac{p(x)}{q(x)}$, set equal to a value, where $p(x)$ and $q(x)$ are both polynomials. Notice that a rational equation has an equal sign, which is different from expressions. This leads to solutions, or numbers that make the equation true.

It is possible to solve rational equations by trying to get all of the *x* terms out of the denominator and then isolate them on one side of the equation. For example, to solve the equation $\frac{3x+2}{2x+3} = 4$, start by multiplying both sides by $(2x + 3)$. This will cancel on the left side to yield $3x + 2 = 4(2x + 3)$, then $3x + 2 = 8x + 12$. Now, subtract $8x$ from both sides, which yields $-5x + 2 = 12$. Subtracting 2 from both sides results in $-5x = 10$. Finally, divide both sides by -5 to obtain $x = -2$.

Sometimes, when solving rational equations, it can be easier to try to simplify the rational expression by factoring the numerator and denominator first, then cancelling out common factors. For example, to solve $\frac{2x^2-8x+6}{x^2-3x+2} = 1$, start by factoring $2x^2 - 8x + 6 = 2(x^2 - 4x + 3) = 2(x - 1)(x - 3)$. Then, factor $x^2 - 3x + 2$ into $(x - 1)(x - 2)$. This turns the original equation into:

$$\frac{2(x-1)(x-3)}{(x-1)(x-2)} = 1$$

The common factor of $(x - 1)$ can be canceled, leaving us with $\frac{2(x-3)}{x-2} = 1$. Now the same method used in the previous example can be followed. Multiplying both sides by $x - 2$ and performing the multiplication on the left yields $2x - 6 = x - 2$, which can be simplified to $x = 4$.

Rational Functions

A rational function is similar to an equation, but it includes two variables. In general, a rational function is in the form: $f(x) = \frac{p(x)}{q(x)}$, where $p(x)$ and $q(x)$ are polynomials. Refer to the previous Functions section for a more detailed definition of functions. Rational functions are defined everywhere except where the denominator is equal to zero. When the denominator is equal to zero, this indicates either a hole in the graph or an asymptote. An asymptote can be either vertical, horizontal, or slant. A hole occurs when both the numerator and denominator are equal to 0 for a given value of *x*. A rational function can have at most one vertical asymptote and one horizontal or slant asymptote. An asymptote is a line such that the distance between the curve and the line tends toward 0, but never reaches it, as the line heads toward infinity. Examples of these types of functions are shown below. The first graph shows a rational function with a vertical asymptote at x = 0. This can be found by setting the denominator equal to 0. In this case it is just x = 0.

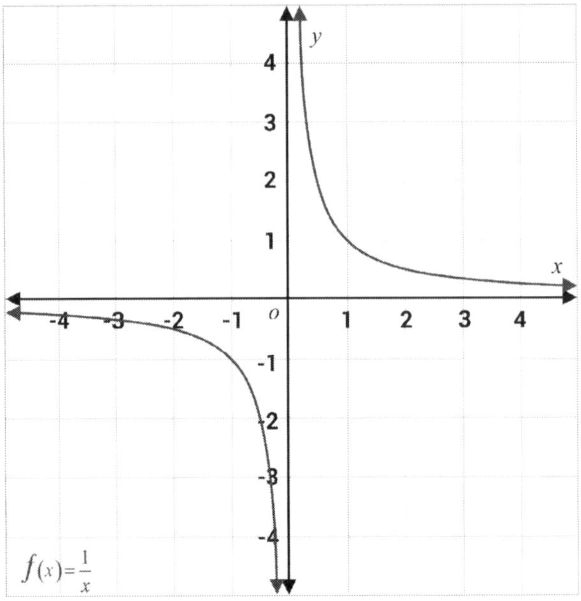

The second graph shows a rational function with a vertical asymptote at x = -.5. Again this can be found by just setting the denominator equal to 0. So, $2x^2 + x = 0, 2x + 1 = 0, 2x = -1, x = -.5$. This graph also has a hole in the graph at $x = 0$. This is because both the numerator and denominator are equal to 0 when $x = 0$.

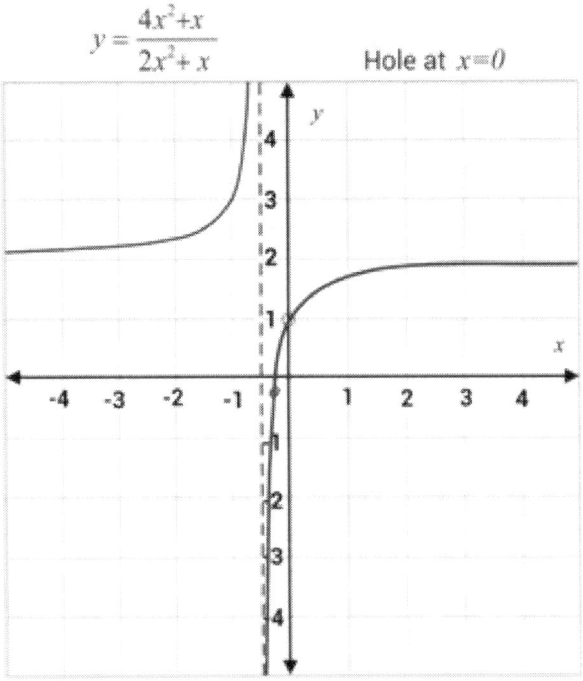

Practice Questions

1. What is the value of b in this equation?

$5b - 4 = 2b + 17$

a. 13
b. 24
c. 7
d. 21
e. 9

2. Which equation is not a function?

a. $y = |x|$
b. $y = \sqrt{x}$
c. $x = 3$
d. $y = 4$
e. $y = x$

3. What is the product of the following expression?

$$(4x - 8)(5x^2 + x + 6)$$

a. $20x^3 - 36x^2 + 16x - 48$
b. $6x^3 - 41x^2 + 12x + 15$
c. $204 + 11x^2 - 37x - 12$
d. $2x^3 - 11x^2 - 32x + 20$
e. $20x^3 - 40x^2 + 24x - 48$

4. What is the solution for the following equation?

$$\frac{x^2 + x - 30}{x - 5} = 11$$

a. $x = -6$
b. There is no solution.
c. $x = 16$
d. $x = 5$
e. $x = -5$

5. The phone bill is calculated each month using the equation $c = 50g + 75$. The cost of the phone bill per month is represented by c, and g represents the gigabytes of data used that month. What is the value and interpretation of the slope of this equation?

a. 75 dollars per day
b. 75 gigabytes per day
c. 50 dollars per day
d. 50 dollars per gigabyte
e. The slope cannot be determined.

6. What is the solution for the equation $\tan(x) + 1 = 0$, where $0 \leq x < 2\pi$?

a. $x = \frac{3\pi}{4}, \frac{5\pi}{4}$

b. $x = \frac{3\pi}{4}, \frac{\pi}{4}$

c. $x = \frac{5\pi}{4}, \frac{7\pi}{4}$

d. $x = \frac{3\pi}{4}, \frac{7\pi}{4}$

e. $x = \frac{5\pi}{4}, \frac{\pi}{4}$

7. How could the following function be rewritten to identify the zeros?

$$y = 3x^3 + 3x^2 - 18x$$

a. $y = 3x(x+3)(x-2)$
b. $y = x(x-2)(x+3)$
c. $y = 3x(x-3)(x+2)$
d. $y = (x+3)(x-2)$
e. $y = 3x(x+3)(x+2)$

8. Suppose $\frac{x+2}{x} = 2$. What is *x*?

a. -1
b. 0
c. 2
d. 4
e. 1

9. A particle moves along the x-axis so that at any time $t \geq 0$, its velocity is given by $v(t) = \frac{6}{t+3}$. What is the acceleration of the particle at time $t = 5$?

a. $-\frac{2}{3}$
b. $-\frac{3}{16}$
c. $\frac{3}{4}$
d. $\frac{2}{3}$
e. $-\frac{3}{32}$

10. What type of function is modeled by the values in the following table?

X	f(x)
1	2
2	4
3	8
4	16
5	32

a. Linear
b. Exponential
c. Quadratic
d. Cubic
e. Logarithmic

11. An investment of $2,000 is made into an account with an annual interest rate of 5%, compounded continuously. What is the total value for the investment after eight years?

a. $4,707
b. $3,000
c. $2,983.65
d. $10,919.63
e. $1,977.61

12. A line passes through the point (1, 2) and crosses the *y*-axis at *y* = 1. Which of the following is an equation for this line?

a. $y = 2x$
b. $y = x - 1$
c. $x + y = 1$
d. $y = \frac{x}{2} - 2$
e. $y = x + 1$

13. Katie works at a clothing company and sold 192 shirts over the weekend. $\frac{1}{3}$ of the shirts that were sold were patterned, and the rest were solid. Which mathematical expression would calculate the number of solid shirts Katie sold over the weekend?

a. $192 \times \frac{1}{3}$
b. $192 \div \frac{1}{3}$
c. $192 \times (1 - \frac{1}{3})$
d. $192 \div 3$
e. $192 \times (-\frac{1}{3})$

14. The graph shows the position of a car over a 10-second time interval. Which of the following is the correct interpretation of the graph for the interval 1 to 3 seconds?

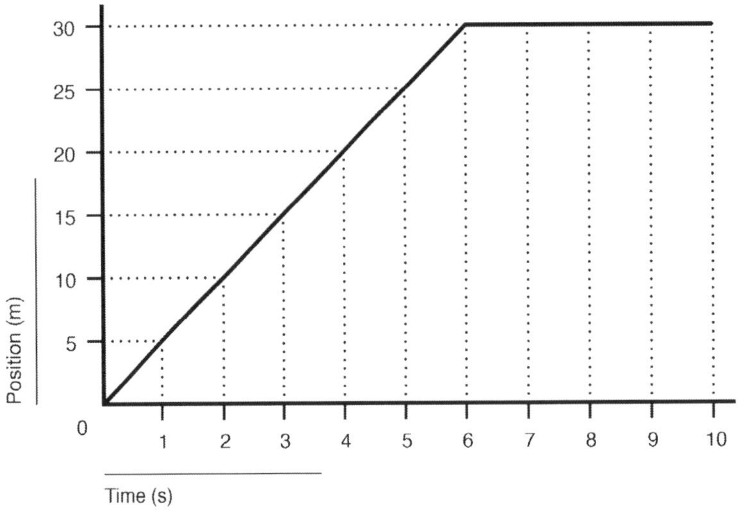

a. The car remains in the same position.
b. The car is traveling at a speed of 5m/s.
c. The car is traveling up a hill.
d. The car is traveling at 5mph.
e. The car accelerates at a rate of 5m/s.

15. Which of the following is the result of simplifying the expression:

$$\frac{4a^{-1}b^{3}}{a^{4}b^{-2}} * \frac{3a}{b}$$

a. $12a^3b^5$

b. $12\frac{b^2}{a^2}$

c. $\frac{12}{a^4}$

d. $7\frac{b^4}{a}$

e. $12\frac{b^4}{a^4}$

16. What are the zeros of the function: $f(x) = x^3 + 4x^2 + 4x$?
a. -2
b. 0, -2
c. 2
d. 0, 2
e. 0

17. What is the solution to the following system of equations?

$$x^2 - 2x + y = 8$$
$$x - y = -2$$

a. $(-2, 3)$
b. There is no solution.
c. $(-2, 0)\ (1, 3)$
d. $(-2, 0)\ (3, 5)$
e. $(2, 0)\ (-1, 3)$

18. Which of the following shows the correct result of simplifying the following expression:

$$(7n + 3n^3 + 3) + (8n + 5n^3 + 2n^4)$$

a. $9n^4 + 15n - 2$
b. $2n^4 + 5n^3 + 15n - 2$
c. $9n^4 + 8n^3 + 15n$
d. $2n^4 + 8n^3 + 15n + 3$
e. $2n^4 + 5n^3 + 15n - 3$

19. How could the following equation be factored to find the zeros?

$$y = x^3 - 3x^2 - 4x$$

a. $0 = x^2(x - 4), x = 0, 4$
b. $0 = 3x(x + 1)(x + 4), x = 0, -1, -4$
c. $0 = x(x + 1)(x + 6), x = 0, -1, -6$
d. $0 = 3x(x + 1)(x - 4), x = 0, 1, -4$
e. $0 = x(x + 1)(x - 4), x = 0, -1, 4$

20. What is the simplified quotient of the following expression?

$$\frac{5x^3}{3x^2y} \div \frac{25}{3y^9}$$

a. $\frac{125x}{9y^{10}}$

b. $\frac{x}{5y^8}$

c. $\frac{5}{xy^8}$

d. $\frac{xy^8}{5}$

e. $\frac{xy^2}{5x}$

Answer Explanations

1. C: To solve for the value of b, both sides of the equation need to be equalized.

Start by cancelling out the lower value of -4 by adding 4 to both sides:

5b – 4 = 2b + 17
5*b* – 4 + 4 = 2*b* + 17 + 4
5*b* = 2*b* + 21

The variable *b* is the same on each side, so subtract the lower 2b from each side:

5*b* = 2*b* + 21
5*b* – 2*b* = 2*b* + 21 – 2*b*
3*b* = 21

Then divide both sides by 3 to get the value of *b*:

3*b* = 21

$$\frac{3b}{3} = \frac{21}{3}$$

b = 7

2. C: The equation $x = 3$ is not a function because it does not pass the vertical line test. This test is made from the definition of a function, where each x-value must be mapped to one and only one y-value. This equation is a vertical line, so the x-value of 3 is mapped with an infinite number of y-values.

3. A: Finding the product means distributing one polynomial to the other so that each term in the first is multiplied by each term in the second. Then, like terms can be collected. Multiplying the factors yields the expression $20x^3 + 4x^2 + 24x - 40x^2 - 8x - 48$. Collecting like terms means adding the x^2 terms and adding the x terms. The final answer after simplifying the expression is $20x^3 - 36x^2 + 16x - 48$.

4. B: The equation can be solved by factoring the numerator into $(x + 6)(x - 5)$. Since that same factor $(x - 5)$ exists on top and bottom, that factor cancels. This leaves the equation $x + 6 = 11$. Solving the equation gives the answer $x = 5$. When this value is plugged into the equation, it yields a zero in the denominator of the fraction. Since this is undefined, there is no solution.

5. D: The slope from this equation is 50, and it is interpreted as the cost per gigabyte used. Since the g-value represents number of gigabytes and the equation is set equal to the cost in dollars, the slope relates these two values. For every gigabyte used on the phone, the bill goes up 50 dollars.

6. D: Using SOHCAHTOA, tangent is $\frac{y}{x}$ for the special triangles. Since the value needs to be negative one, the angle must be some form of 45 degrees or $\frac{\pi}{4}$. The value is negative in the second and fourth quadrant, so the answer is $\frac{3\pi}{4}$ and $\frac{7\pi}{4}$.

7. A: The function can be factored to identify the zeros. First, the term $3x$ is factored out to the front because each term contains $3x$. Then, the quadratic is factored into $(x + 3)(x - 2)$.

8. C: Multiply both sides by x to get $x + 2 = 2x$, which simplifies to $-x = -2$, or x = 2.

9. E: The acceleration of the particle can be found by taking the derivative of the velocity equation. This equation is $v'(t) = \frac{0-6(1)}{(t+3)^2} = \frac{-6}{(t+3)^2}$. Finding the acceleration at time $t = 5$ can be found by plugging five in for the variable t in the derivative. The equation and answer are:

$$v'(5) = \frac{-6}{(5+3)^2} = \frac{-6}{64} = \frac{-3}{32}$$

10. B: The table shows values that are increasing exponentially. The differences between the inputs are the same, while the differences in the outputs are changing by a factor of 2. The values in the table can be modeled by the equation $f(x) = 2^x$.

that are the same on the top and bottom cancel out, leaving the simplified expression $\sin\theta$.

11. C: The formula for continually compounded interest is $A = Pe^{rt}$. Plugging in the given values to find the total amount in the account yields the equation:

$$A = 2000e^{0.05*8} = 2983.65$$

12. E: From the slope-intercept form, $y = mx + b$, it is known that b is the y-intercept, which is 1. Compute the slope as $\frac{2-1}{1-0} = 1$, so the equation should be $y = x + 1$.

13. C: $\frac{1}{3}$ of the shirts sold were patterned. Therefore, $1 - \frac{1}{3} = \frac{2}{3}$ of the shirts sold were solid. Anytime "of" a quantity appears in a word problem, multiplication needs to be used. Therefore, $192 \times \frac{2}{3} = 192 \times \frac{2}{3} = \frac{384}{3} = 128$ solid shirts were sold. The entire expression is $192 \times \left(1 - \frac{1}{3}\right)$.

14. B: The car is traveling at a speed of five meters per second. On the interval from one to three seconds, the position changes by fifteen meters. By making this change in position over time into a rate, the speed becomes ten meters in two seconds or five meters in one second.

15. E: To simplify the given equation, the first step is to make all exponents positive by moving them to the opposite place in the fraction. This expression becomes:

$$\frac{4b^3b^2}{a^1a^4} * \frac{3a}{b}$$

Then the rules for exponents can be used to simplify. Multiplying the same bases means the exponents can be added. Dividing the same bases means the exponents are subtracted.

16. B: There are two zeros for the given function. They are $x = 0, -2$. The zeros can be found a number of ways, but this particular equation can be factored into $f(x) = x(x^2 + 4x + 4) = x(x+2)(x+2)$. By setting each factor equal to zero and solving for x, there are two solutions. On a graph, these zeros can be seen where the line crosses the x-axis.

17. D: This system of equations involves one quadratic function and one linear function, as seen from the degree of each equation. One way to solve this is through substitution. Solving for y in the second equation yields $y = x + 2$. Plugging this equation in for the y of the quadratic equation yields $x^2 - 2x + x + 2 = 8$. Simplifying the equation, it becomes $x^2 - x + 2 = 8$. Setting this equal to zero and factoring, it becomes $x^2 - x - 6 = 0 = (x - 3)(x + 2)$. Solving these two factors for x gives the zeros $x = 3, -2$. To find the y-value for the point, each number can be plugged in to either original equation. Solving each one for y yields the points $(3, 5)$ and $(-2, 0)$.

18. D: The expression is simplified by collecting like terms. Terms with the same variable and exponent are like terms, and their coefficients can be added.

19. E: Finding the zeros for a function by factoring is done by setting the equation equal to zero, then completely factoring. Since there was a common x for each term in the provided equation, that is factored out first. Then the quadratic that is left can be factored into two binomials: $(x + 1)(x - 4)$. Setting each factor equation equal to zero and solving for x yields three zeros.

20. D: Dividing rational expressions follows the same rule as dividing fractions. The division is changed to multiplication, and the reciprocal is found in the second fraction. This turns the expression into:

$$\frac{5x^3}{3x^2} * \frac{3y^9}{25}$$

Multiplying across and simplifying, the final expression is $\frac{xy^8}{5}$.

Geometry and Measurement

Euclidean Geometry Versus Non-Euclidean Geometry

The main difference between Euclidean geometry and non-Euclidean geometry is the definition of parallel lines. In Euclidean geometry, given a point and a line that does not contain the given point, there is only one line running through the point that exists in the same plane as the given line but never intersects it. Hyperbolic and elliptic geometry (non-Euclidean) are curved spaces, and in both geometries, there is more than one line that would pass through the given point that are parallel to the given line.

Plane Geometry

Algebraic equations can be used to describe geometric figures in the plane. The method for doing so is to use the *Cartesian coordinate plane*. The idea behind these Cartesian coordinates (named for mathematician and philosopher Descartes) is that from a specific point on the plane, known as the *center*, one can specify any other point by saying *how far to the right or left* and *how far up or down*.

The plane is covered with a grid. The two directions, right to left and bottom to top, are called *axes* (singular *axis*). When working with *x* and *y* variables, the *x* variable corresponds to the right and left axis, and the *y* variable corresponds to the up and down axis.

Any point on the grid is found by specifying how far to travel from the center along the *x*-axis and how far to travel along the *y*-axis. The ordered pair can be written as (x, y). A positive *x* value means go to the right on the *x*-axis, while a negative *x* value means to go to the left. A positive *y* value means to go up, while a negative value means to go down. Several points are shown as examples in the figure.

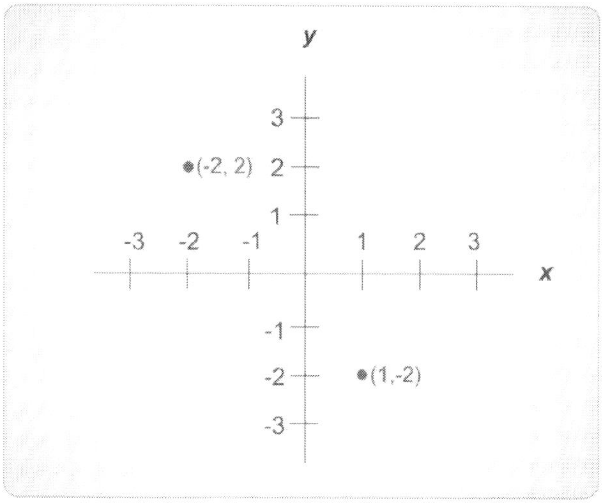

Cartesian Coordinate Plane

The Coordinate Plane

The coordinate plane can be divided into four *quadrants*. The upper-right part of the plane is called the *first quadrant*, where both *x* and *y* are positive. The *second quadrant* is the upper-left, where *x* is negative but *y* is positive. The *third quadrant* is the lower left, where both *x* and *y* are negative. Finally, the *fourth quadrant* is in the lower right, where *x* is positive but *y* is negative. These quadrants are often written with Roman numerals:

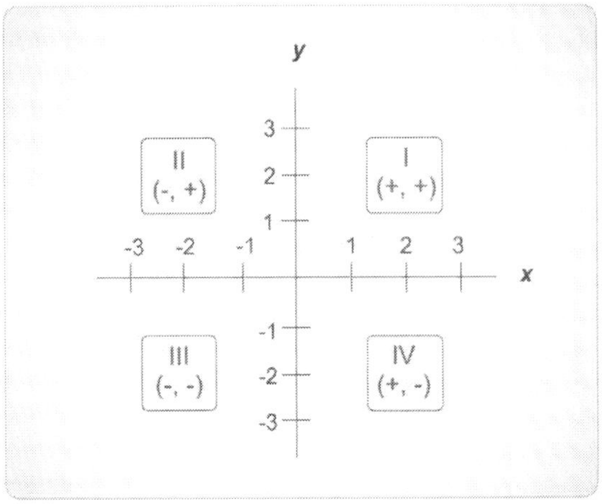

In addition to graphing individual points as shown above, the graph lines and curves in the plane can be graphed corresponding to equations. In general, if there is some equation involving *x* and *y*, then the *graph* of that equation consists of all the points (x, y) in the Cartesian coordinate plane, which satisfy this equation.

Given the equation $y = x + 2$, the point $(0, 2)$ is in the graph, since $2 = 0 + 2$ is a true equation. However, the point $(1, 4)$ will *not* be in the graph, because $4 = 1 + 2$ is false.

Straight Lines

The simplest equations to graph are the equations whose graphs are lines, called *linear equations*. Every linear equation can be rewritten algebraically so that it looks like $Ax + By = C$.

First, the ratio of the change in the *y* coordinate to the change in the *x* coordinate is constant for any two distinct points on the line. In any pair of points on a line, two points, (x_1, y_1) and (x_2, y_2)—

where $x_1 \neq x_2$—the ratio $\frac{y_2 - y_1}{x_2 - x_1}$ will always be the same, even if another pair of points is used.

This ratio, $\frac{y_2 - y_1}{x_2 - x_1}$, is called the *slope* of the line and is often denoted with the letter m. If the slope is *positive*, then the line goes upward when moving to the right. If the slope is *negative*, then it moves downward when moving to the right. If the slope is 0, then the line is *horizontal*, and the *y* coordinate is constant along the entire line. For lines where the *x* coordinate is constant along the entire line, the slope is not defined, and these lines are called *vertical* lines.

The *y* coordinate of the point where the line touches the *y*-axis is called the *y-intercept* of the line. It is often denoted by the letter b, used in the form of the linear equation $y = mx + b$. The *x* coordinate of the point where the line touches the *x*-axis is called the *x-intercept*. It is also called the *zero* of the line.

Suppose two lines have slopes m_1 and m_2. If the slopes are equal, $m_1 = m_2$, then the lines are *parallel*. Parallel lines never meet one another. If $m_1 = -\frac{1}{m_2}$, then the lines are called *perpendicular* or *orthogonal*. Their slopes can also be called opposite reciprocals of each other.

There are several convenient ways to write down linear equations. The common forms are listed here:

Standard Form: $Ax + By = C$, where the slope is given by $\frac{-A}{B}$, and the *y*-intercept is given by $\frac{C}{B}$.

Slope-Intercept Form: $y = mx + b$, where the slope is *m,* and the *y*-intercept is *b.*

Point-Slope Form: $y - y_1 = m(x - x_1)$, where *m* is the slope, and (x_1, y_1) is any point on the line.

Two-Point Form: $\frac{y-y_1}{x-x_1} = \frac{y_2-y_1}{x_2-x_1}$, where (x_1, y_1), and (x_2, y_2) are any two distinct points on the line.

Intercept Form: $\frac{x}{x_1} + \frac{y}{y_1} = 1$, where x_1 is the *x*-intercept, and y_1 is the *y*-intercept.

Depending upon the given information, different forms of the linear equation can be easier to write down than others. When given two points, the two-point form is easy to write down. If the slope and a single point is known, the point-slope form is easiest to start with. In general, which form to start with depends upon the given information.

Solving Line Problems

Two lines are parallel if they have the same slope and different intercept. Two lines are perpendicular if the product of their slope equals -1. Parallel lines never intersect unless they are the same line, and perpendicular lines intersect at a right angle. If two lines aren't parallel, they must intersect at one point. Determining equations of lines based on properties of parallel and perpendicular lines appears in word problems. To find an equation of a line, both the slope and a point the line goes through are necessary. Therefore, if an equation of a line is needed that's parallel to a given line and runs through a specified point, the slope of the given line and the point are plugged into the point-slope form of an equation of a line. Secondly, if an equation of a line is needed that's perpendicular to a given line running through a specified point, the negative reciprocal of the slope of the given line and the point are plugged into the point-slope form. Also, if the point of intersection of two lines is known, that point will be used to solve the set of equations. Therefore, to solve a system of equations, the point of intersection must be found. If a set of two equations with two unknown variables has no solution, the lines are parallel.

Relationships between Angles

Supplementary angles add up to 180 degrees. *Vertical angles* are two nonadjacent angles formed by two intersecting lines. *Corresponding angles* are two angles in the same position whenever a straight line (known as a *transversal*) crosses two others. If the two lines are parallel, the corresponding angles are equal. *Alternate interior angles* are also a pair of angles formed when two lines are crossed by a transversal. They are opposite angles that exist inside of the two lines. In the corresponding angles diagram above, angles 2 and 7 are alternate interior angles, as well as angles 6 and 3. *Alternate exterior angles* are opposite angles formed by a transversal but, in contrast to interior angles, exterior angles exist outside the two original lines. Therefore, angles 1 and 8 are alternate exterior angles and so are angles 5 and 4. Finally, *consecutive interior angles* are pairs of angles formed by a transversal. These angles are located on the same side of the transversal and inside the two original lines. Therefore, angles 2 and 3 are a pair of consecutive interior angles, and so are angles 6 and 7. These definitions are instrumental in solving many problems that involve determining relationships between angles.

Conics

The graph of an equation of the form $y = ax^2 + bx + c$ or $x = ay^2 + by + c$ is called a *parabola*.

The graph of an equation of the form $\frac{x^2}{a^2} - \frac{y^2}{b^2} = 1$ or $-\frac{x^2}{a^2} + \frac{y^2}{b^2} = 1$ is called a *hyperbola*.

The graph of an equation of the form $\frac{(x-x_0)^2}{a^2} + \frac{(y-y_0)^2}{b^2} = 1$ is called an *ellipse*. If $a = b$ then this is a circle with *radius* $r = \frac{1}{a}$.

Sets of Points in the Plane

The *midpoint* between two points, (x_1, y_1) and (x_2, y_2), is given by taking the average of the *x* coordinates and the average of the *y* coordinates: $\left(\frac{x_1+x_2}{2}, \frac{y_1+y_2}{2}\right)$.

The *distance* between two points, (x_1, y_1) and (x_2, y_2), is given by the *Pythagorean formula*, $\sqrt{(x_2 - x_1)^2 + (y_2 - y_1)^2}$.

To find the perpendicular distance between a line $Ax + By = C$ and a point (x_1, y_1) not on the line, we need to use the formula:

$$\frac{|Ax_1 + By_1 + C|}{\sqrt{A^2 + B^2}}$$

Symmetry

Using the types of transformations above, if an object can undergo these changes and not appear to have changed, then the figure is symmetrical. If an object can be split in half by a line and flipped over that line to lie directly on top of itself, it is said to have *line symmetry*. An example of both types of figures is seen below.

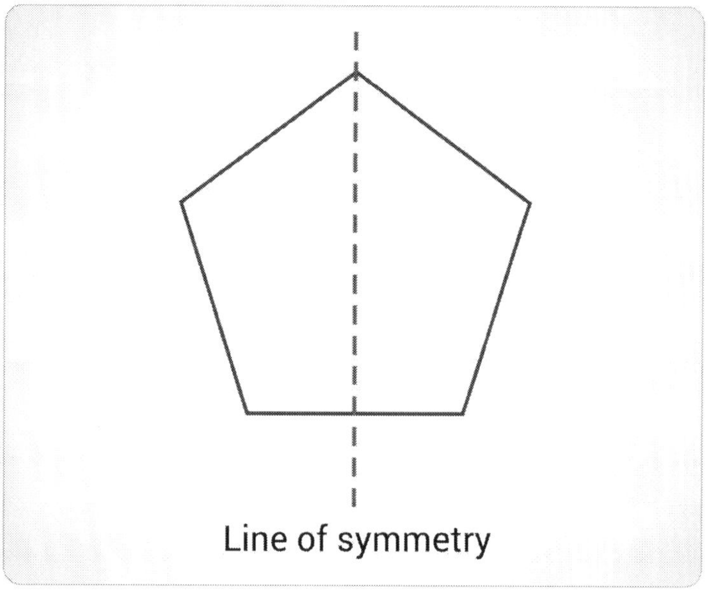

If an object can be rotated about its center to any degree smaller than 360, and it lies directly on top of itself, the object is said to have *rotational symmetry*. An example of this type of symmetry is shown below. The pentagon has an order of 5.

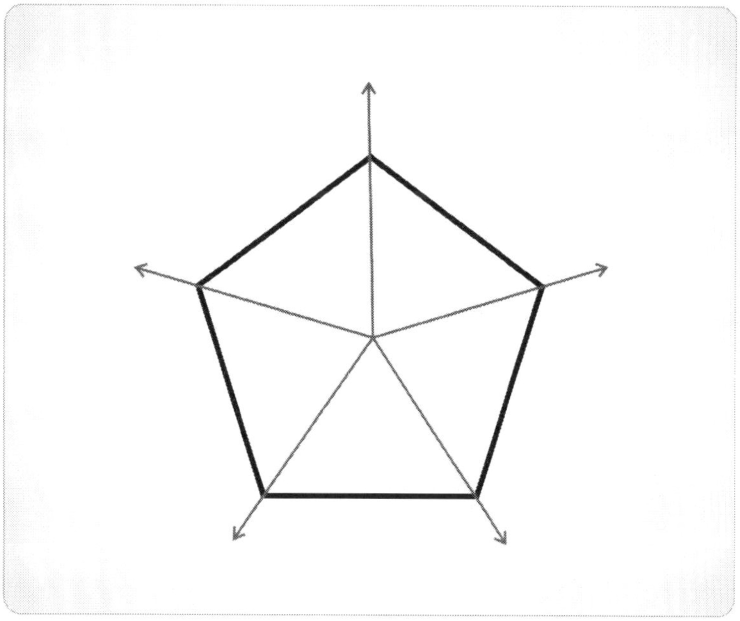

The rotational symmetry lines in the figure above can be used to find the angles formed at the center of the pentagon. Knowing that all of the angles together form a full circle, at 360 degrees, the figure can be split into 5 angles equally. By dividing the 360° by 5, each angle is 72°.

Given the length of one side of the figure, the perimeter of the pentagon can also be found using rotational symmetry. If one side length was 3 cm, that side length can be rotated onto each other side length four times. This would give a total of 5 side lengths equal to 3 cm. To find the perimeter, or distance around the figure, multiply 3 by 5. The perimeter of the figure would be 15 cm.

If a line cannot be drawn anywhere on the object to flip the figure onto itself or rotated less than or equal to 180 degrees to lay on top of itself, the object is asymmetrical. Examples of these types of figures are shown below.

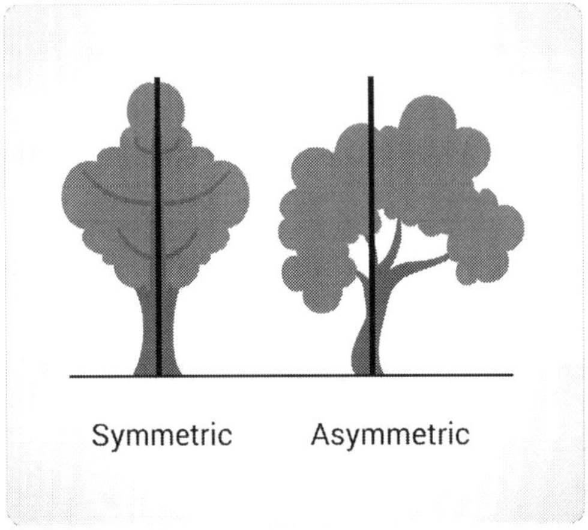

Transformations of a Plane

Given a figure drawn on a plane, many changes can be made to that figure, including *rotation*, *translation*, and *reflection*. Rotations turn the figure about a point, translations slide the figure, and reflections flip the figure over a specified line. When performing these transformations, the original figure is called the *pre-image*, and the figure after transformation is called the *image*.

More specifically, *translation* means that all points in the figure are moved in the same direction by the same distance. In other words, the figure is slid in some fixed direction. Of course, while the entire figure is slid by the same distance, this does not change any of the measurements of the figures involved. The result will have the same distances and angles as the original figure.

In terms of Cartesian coordinates, a translation means a shift of each of the original points (x, y) by a fixed amount in the x and y directions, to become $(x + a, y + b)$.

Another procedure that can be performed is called *reflection*. To do this, a line in the plane is specified, called the *line of reflection*. Then, take each point and flip it over the line so that it is the same distance from the line but on the opposite side of it. This does not change any of the distances or angles involved, but it does reverse the order in which everything appears.

To reflect something over the *x*-axis, the points (x, y) are sent to $(x, -y)$. To reflect something over the *y*-axis, the points (x, y) are sent to the points $(-x, y)$. Flipping over other lines is not something easy to express in Cartesian coordinates. However, by drawing the figure and the line of reflection, the distance to the line and the original points can be used to find the reflected figure.

Example: Reflect this triangle with vertices (-1, 0), (2, 1), and (2, 0) over the *y*-axis. The pre-image is shown below.

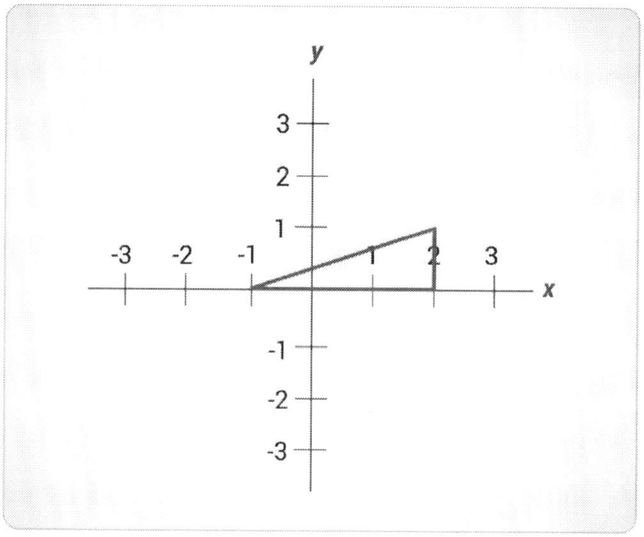

To do this, flip the *x* values of the points involved to the negatives of themselves, while keeping the *y* values the same. The image is shown here.

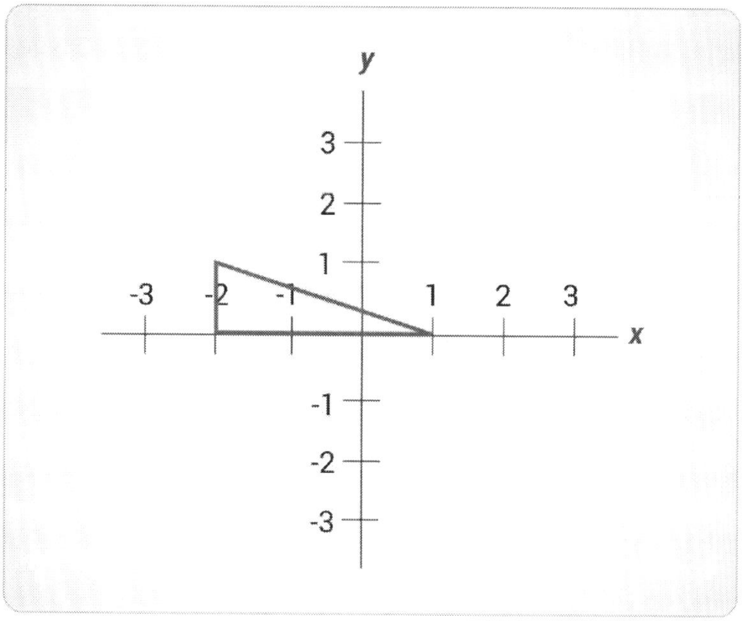

The new vertices will be (1, 0), (-2, 1), and (-2, 0).

Another procedure that does not change the distances and angles in a figure is *rotation*. In this procedure, pick a center point, then rotate every vertex along a circle around that point by the same angle. This procedure is also not easy to express in Cartesian coordinates, and this is not a requirement on this test. However, as with reflections, it's helpful to draw the figures and see what the result of the rotation would look like. This transformation can be performed using a compass and protractor.

Each one of these transformations can be performed on the coordinate plane without changes to the original dimensions or angles.

If two figures in the plane involve the same distances and angles, they are called *congruent figures*. In other words, two figures are congruent when they go from one form to another through reflection, rotation, and translation, or a combination of these.

Remember that rotation and translation will give back a new figure that is identical to the original figure, but reflection will give back a mirror image of it.

To recognize that a figure has undergone a rotation, check to see that the figure has not been changed into a mirror image, but that its orientation has changed (that is, whether the parts of the figure now form different angles with the *x* and *y* axes).

To recognize that a figure has undergone a translation, check to see that the figure has not been changed into a mirror image, and that the orientation remains the same.

To recognize that a figure has undergone a reflection, check to see that the new figure is a mirror image of the old figure.

Keep in mind that sometimes a combination of translations, reflections, and rotations may be performed on a figure.

Dilation

A *dilation* is a transformation that preserves angles, but not distances. This can be thought of as stretching or shrinking a figure. If a dilation makes figures larger, it is called an *enlargement*. If a dilation makes figures smaller, it is called a *reduction*. The easiest example is to dilate around the origin. In this case, multiply the *x* and *y* coordinates by a *scale factor*, k, sending points (x, y) to (kx, ky).

As an example, draw a dilation of the following triangle, whose vertices will be the points (-1, 0), (1, 0), and (1, 1).

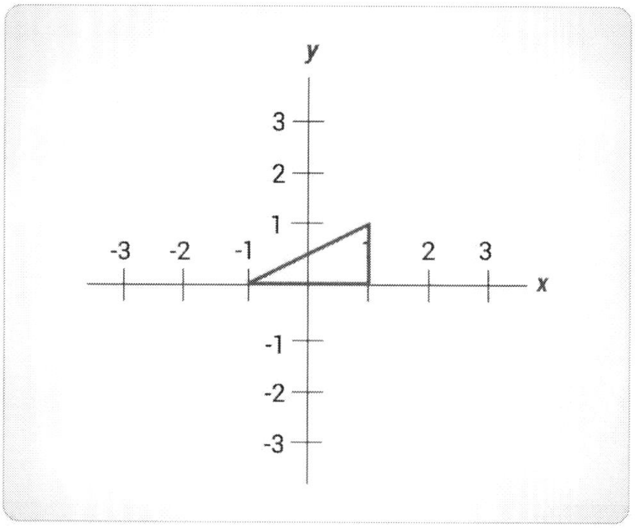

For this problem, dilate by a scale factor of 2, so the new vertices will be (-2, 0), (2, 0), and (2, 2).

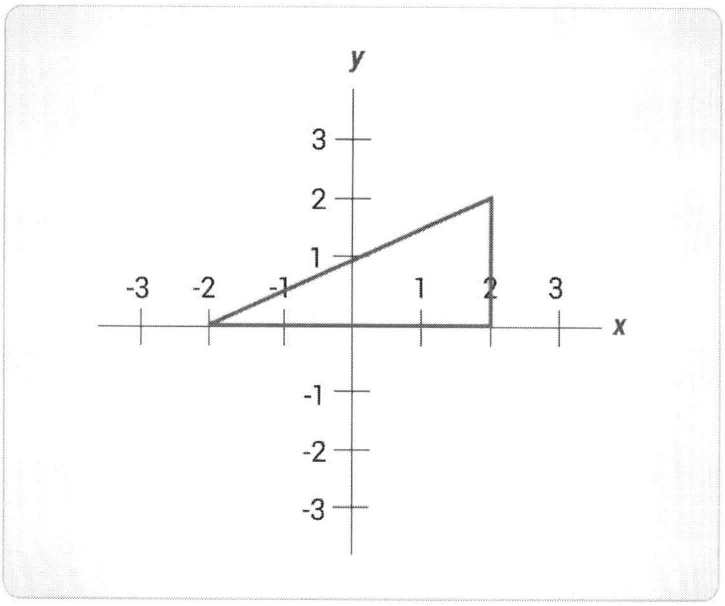

Note that after a dilation, the distances between the vertices of the figure will have changed, but the angles remain the same. The two figures that are obtained by dilation, along with possibly translation, rotation, and reflection, are all *similar* to one another. Another way to think of this is that similar figures have the same number of vertices and edges, and their angles are all the same. Similar figures have the same basic shape, but are different in size.

Perimeters and Areas

The *perimeter* of a polygon is the total length of a trip around the whole polygon, starting and ending at the same point. It is found by adding up the lengths of each line segment in the polygon. For a rectangle with sides of length *x* and *y*, the perimeter will be $2x + 2y$.

The area of a polygon is the area of the region that it encloses. Regarding the area of a rectangle with sides of length *x* and *y*, the area is given by xy. For a triangle with a base of length *b* and a height of length *h*, the area is $\frac{1}{2}bh$.

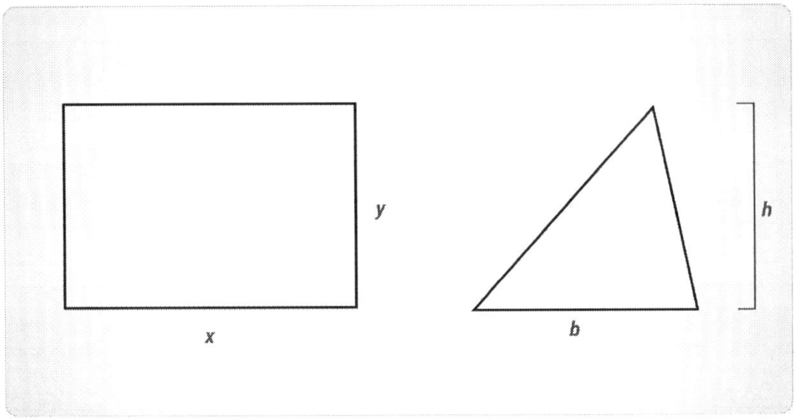

To find the areas of more general polygons, it is usually easiest to break up the polygon into rectangles and triangles. For example, find the area of the following figure whose vertices are (-1, 0), (-1, 2), (1, 3), and (1, 0).

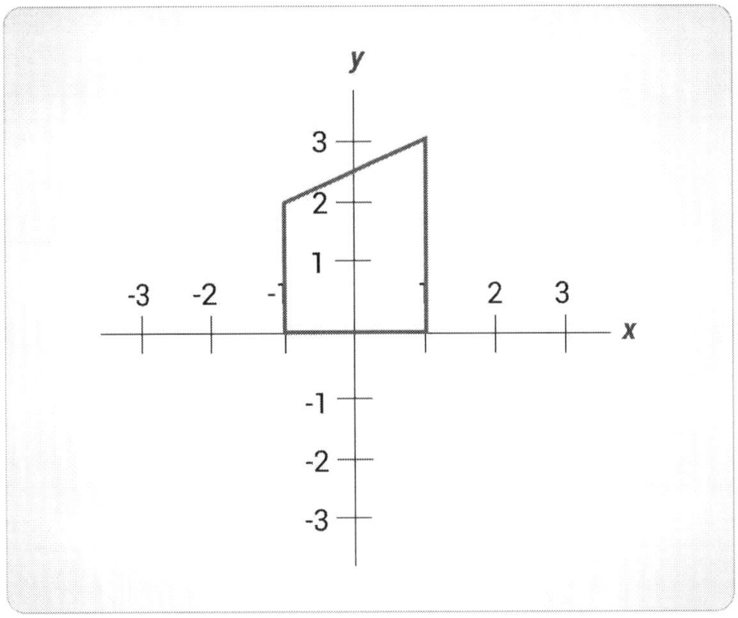

Separate this into a rectangle and a triangle as shown:

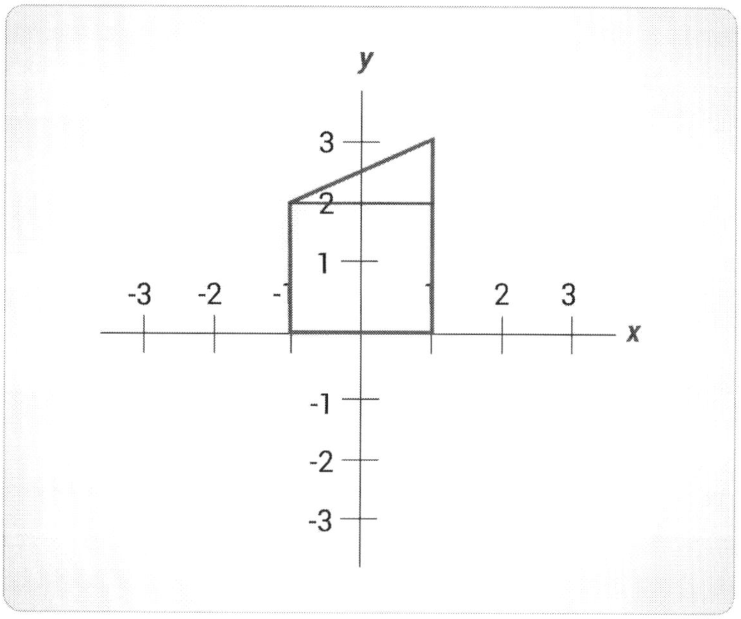

The rectangle has a height of 2 and a width of 2, so it has a total area of $2 \cdot 2 = 4$. The triangle has a width of 2 and a height of 1, so it has an area of $\frac{1}{2} 2 \cdot 1 = 1$. Therefore, the entire quadrilateral has an area of 4 + 1 = 5.

As another example, suppose someone wants to tile a rectangular room that is 10 feet by 6 feet using triangular tiles that are 12 inches by 6 inches. How many tiles would be needed? To figure this, first find the area of the room, which will be $10 \cdot 6 = 60$ square feet. The dimensions of the triangle are 1 foot by ½ foot, so the area of each triangle is $\frac{1}{2} \cdot 1 \cdot \frac{1}{2} = \frac{1}{4}$ square feet. Notice that the dimensions of the triangle had to be converted to the same units as the rectangle. Now, take the total area divided by the area of one tile to find the answer: $\frac{60}{\frac{1}{4}} = 60 \cdot 4 = 240$ tiles required.

Three-Dimensional Solids

A solid figure, or simply solid, is a figure that encloses a part of space. Some solids consist of flat surfaces only while others include curved surfaces. Solid figures are often defined as three-dimensional shapes. Common three-dimensional shapes include spheres, prisms, cubes, pyramids, cylinders, and cones.

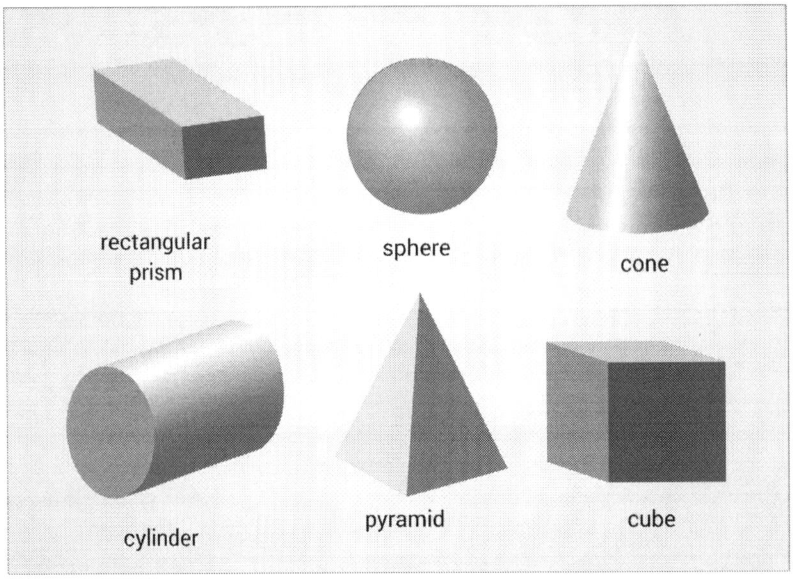

Volumes and Surface Areas

Geometry in three dimensions is similar to geometry in two dimensions. The main new feature is that three points now define a unique *plane* that passes through each of them. Three dimensional objects can be made by putting together two dimensional figures in different surfaces. Below, some of the possible three dimensional figures will be provided, along with formulas for their volumes and surface areas.

A rectangular prism is a box whose sides are all rectangles meeting at 90° angles. Such a box has three dimensions: length, width, and height. If the length is *x*, the width is *y*, and the height is *z*, then the volume is given by $V = xyz$.

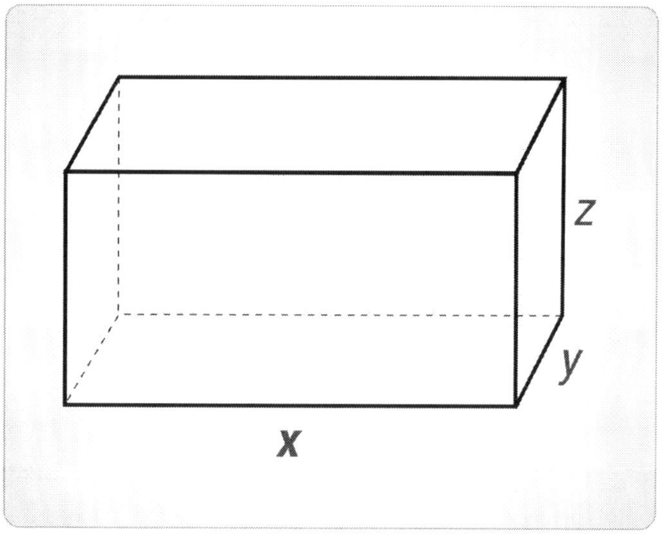

The surface area will be given by computing the surface area of each rectangle and adding them together. There are a total of six rectangles. Two of them have sides of length *x* and *y*, two have sides of length *y* and *z*, and two have sides of length *x* and *z*. Therefore, the total surface area will be given by $SA = 2xy + 2yz + 2xz$.

A *rectangular pyramid* is a figure with a rectangular base and four triangular sides that meet at a single vertex. If the rectangle has sides of length *x* and *y*, then the volume will be given by $V = \frac{1}{3}xyh$.

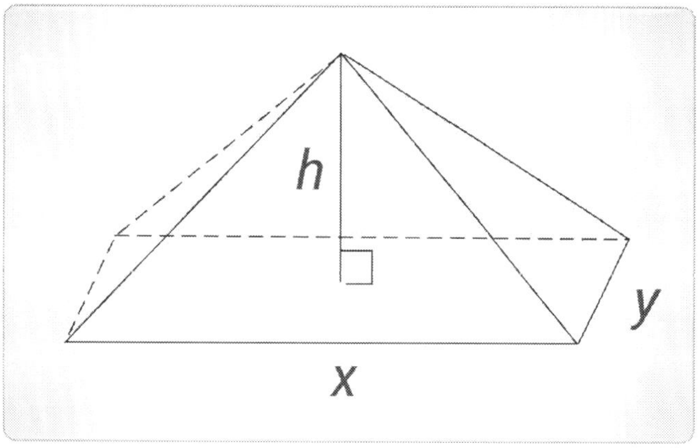

To find the surface area, the dimensions of each triangle need to be known. However, these dimensions can differ depending on the problem in question. Therefore, there is no general formula for calculating total surface area.

A *sphere* is a set of points all of which are equidistant from some central point. It is like a circle, but in three dimensions. The volume of a sphere of radius *r* is given by $V = \frac{4}{3}\pi r^3$. The surface area is given by $A = 4\pi r^2$.

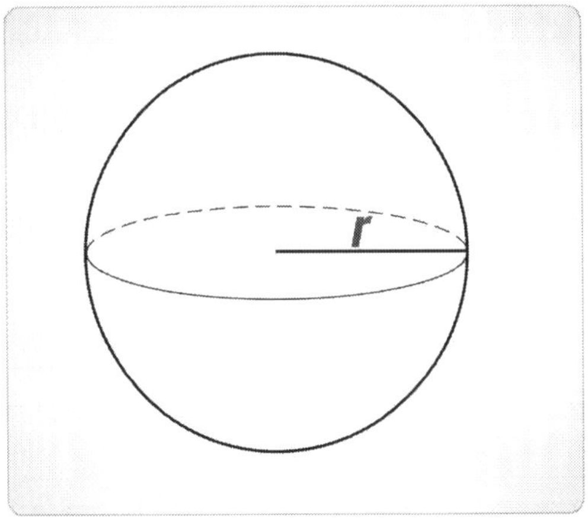

The Pythagorean Theorem

The Pythagorean theorem is an important result in geometry. It states that for right triangles, the sum of the squares of the two shorter sides will be equal to the square of the longest side (also called the *hypotenuse*). The longest side will always be the side opposite to the 90° angle. If this side is called *c*, and the other two sides are *a* and *b*, then the Pythagorean theorem states that $c^2 = a^2 + b^2$. Since lengths are always positive, this also can be written as $c = \sqrt{a^2 + b^2}$.

A diagram to show the parts of a triangle using the Pythagorean theorem is below.

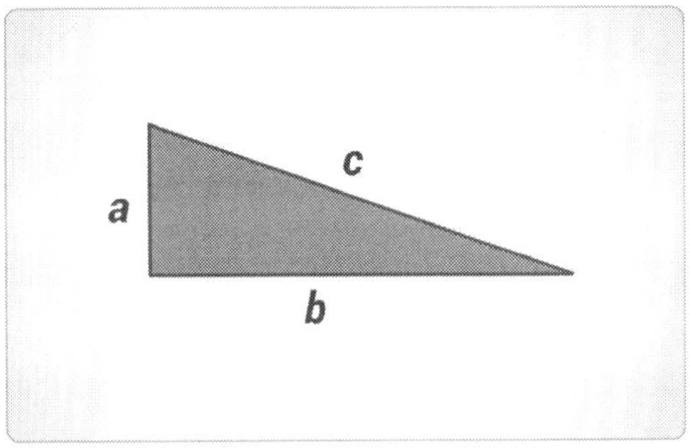

As an example of the theorem, suppose that Shirley has a rectangular field that is 5 feet wide and 12 feet long, and she wants to split it in half using a fence that goes from one corner to the opposite corner. How long will this fence need to be? To figure this out, note that this makes the field into two right triangles, whose hypotenuse will be the fence dividing it in half. Therefore, the fence length will be given by $\sqrt{5^2 + 12^2} = \sqrt{169} = 13$ feet long.

Similar Figures and Proportions

Sometimes, two figures are similar, meaning they have the same basic shape and the same interior angles, but they have different dimensions. If the ratio of two corresponding sides is known, then that ratio, or scale factor, holds true for all of the dimensions of the new figure.

Here is an example of applying this principle. Suppose that Lara is 5 feet tall and is standing 30 feet from the base of a light pole, and her shadow is 6 feet long. How high is the light on the pole? To figure this, it helps to make a sketch of the situation:

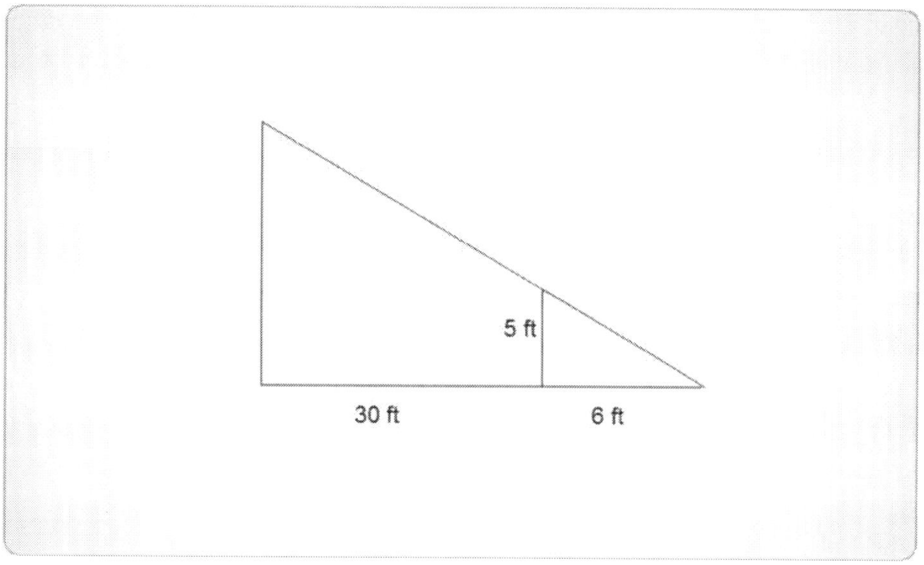

The light pole is the left side of the triangle. Lara is the 5-foot vertical line. Notice that there are two right triangles here, and that they have all the same angles as one another. Therefore, they form similar triangles. So, figure the ratio of proportionality between them.

The bases of these triangles are known. The small triangle, formed by Lara and her shadow, has a base of 6 feet. The large triangle, formed by the light pole along with the line from the base of the pole out to the end of Lara's shadow is $30 + 6 = 36$ feet long. So, the ratio of the big triangle to the little triangle will be $\frac{36}{6} = 6$. The height of the little triangle is 5 feet. Therefore, the height of the big triangle will be $6 \cdot 5 = 30$ feet, meaning that the light is 30 feet up the pole.

Notice that the perimeter of a figure changes by the ratio of proportionality between two similar figures, but the area changes by the *square* of the ratio. This is because if the length of one side is doubled, the area is quadrupled.

As an example, suppose two rectangles are similar, but the edges of the second rectangle are three times longer than the edges of the first rectangle. The area of the first rectangle is 10 square inches. How much more area does the second rectangle have than the first?

To answer this, note that the area of the second rectangle is $3^2 = 9$ times the area of the first rectangle, which is 10 square inches. Therefore, the area of the second rectangle is going to be $9 \cdot 10 = 90$ square inches. This means it has $90 - 10 = 80$ square inches more area than the first rectangle.

As a second example, suppose X and Y are similar right triangles. The hypotenuse of X is 4 inches. The area of Y is $\frac{1}{4}$ the area of X. What is the hypotenuse of Y?

First, realize the area has changed by a factor of $\frac{1}{4}$. The area changes by a factor that is the *square* of the ratio of changes in lengths, so the ratio of the lengths is the square root of the ratio of areas. That means that the ratio of lengths must be is $\sqrt{\frac{1}{4}} = \frac{1}{2}$, and the hypotenuse of Y must be $\frac{1}{2} \cdot 4 = 2$ inches.

Volumes between similar solids change like the cube of the change in the lengths of their edges. Likewise, if the ratio of the volumes between similar solids is known, the ratio between their lengths is known by finding the cube root of the ratio of their volumes.

For example, suppose there are two similar rectangular pyramids X and Y. The base of X is 1 inch by 2 inches, and the volume of X is 8 inches. The volume of Y is 64 inches. What are the dimensions of the base of Y?

To answer this, first find the ratio of the volume of Y to the volume of X. This will be given by $\frac{64}{8} = 8$. Now the ratio of lengths is the cube root of the ratio of volumes, or $\sqrt[3]{8} = 2$. So, the dimensions of the base of Y must be 2 inches by 4 inches.

Trigonometric Functions

Trigonometric functions are also used to describe behavior in mathematics. *Trigonometry* is the relationship between the angles and sides of a triangle. *Trigonometric functions* include sine, cosine, tangent, secant, cosecant, and cotangent. The functions are defined through ratios in a right triangle. SOHCAHTOA is a common acronym used to remember these ratios, which are defined by the relationships of the sides and angles relative to the right angle. Sine is opposite over hypotenuse, cosine is adjacent over hypotenuse, and tangent is opposite over adjacent. These ratios are the reciprocals of secant, cosecant, and cotangent, respectively. Angles can be measured in degrees or radians. Here is a diagram of SOHCAHTOA:

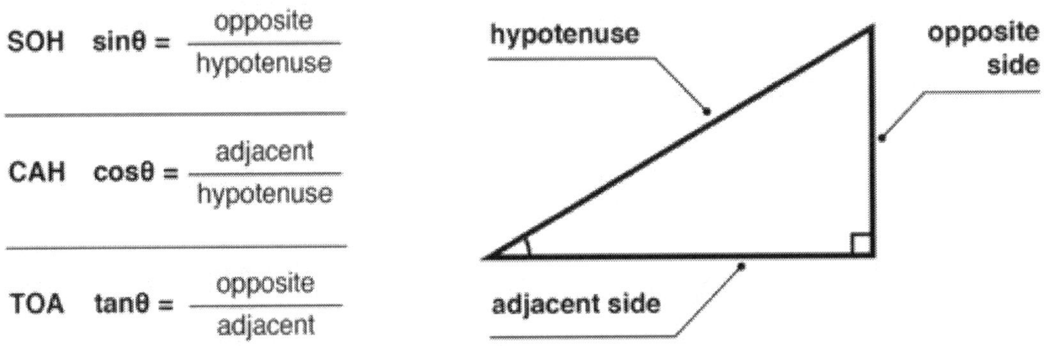

A *radian* is equal to the angle that subtends the arc with the same length as the radius of the circle. It is another unit for measuring angles, in addition to degrees. The unit circle is used to describe different radian measurements and the trigonometric ratios for special angles. The circle has a center at the origin, $(0, 0)$, and a radius of 1, which can be seen below. The points where the circle crosses an axis are labeled.

The circle begins on the right-hand side of the x-axis at 0 radians. Since the circumference of a circle is $2\pi r$ and the radius $r = 1$, the circumference is 2π. Zero and 2π are labeled as radian measurements at the point $(1, 0)$ on the graph. The radian measures around the rest of the circle are labeled also in relation to π; π is at the point $(-1, 0)$, also known as 180 degrees. Since these two measurements are equal, $\pi = 180$ degrees written as a ratio can be used to convert degrees to radians or vice versa. For example, to convert 30 degrees to radians, $30 \text{ degrees} * \frac{\pi}{180 \text{ degrees}}$ can be used to obtain $\frac{1}{6}\pi$ or $\frac{\pi}{6}$. This radian measure is a point the unit circle

The coordinates labeled on the unit circle are found based on two common right triangles. The ratios formed in the coordinates can be found using these triangles. Each of these triangles can be inserted into the circle to correspond 30, 45, and 60 degrees or $\frac{\pi}{6}, \frac{\pi}{4}$, and $\frac{\pi}{3}$ radians.

By letting the hypotenuse length of these triangles equal 1, these triangles can be placed inside the unit circle. These coordinates can be used to find the trigonometric ratio for any of the radian measurements on the circle.

Given any (x, y) on the unit circle, $\sin(\theta) = y$, $\cos(\theta) = x$, and $\tan(\theta) = \frac{y}{x}$. The value θ is the angle that spans the arc around the unit circle. For example, finding $\sin(\frac{\pi}{4})$ means finding the y-value corresponding to the angle $\theta = \frac{\pi}{4}$. The answer is $\frac{\sqrt{2}}{2}$. Finding $\cos(\frac{\pi}{3})$ means finding the x-value corresponding to the angle $\theta = \frac{\pi}{3}$. The answer is $\frac{1}{2}$ or 0.5. Both angles lie in the first quadrant of the unit circle. Trigonometric ratios can also be calculated for radian measures past $\frac{\pi}{2}$, or 90 degrees. Since the same special angles can be moved around the circle, the results only differ with a change in sign. This can be seen at two points labeled in the second and third quadrant.

<u>Representations of Trigonometric Functions</u>

Besides their function form, trigonometric and inverse trigonometric functions can be represented in other various formats. Regardless of the form in which they are given – such as in a table, list of numbers, or graph – it is important to note their periodic tendencies. They all return to the same function values over regular intervals in the domain. Other important concepts to notice in the various formats are range and asymptotes. Many trigonometric functions have a minimum and maximum value, but some have vertical asymptotes at regular intervals, in which the function blows up. All of these properties can be seen in any representation of such functions.

<u>Properties of Trigonometric Functions</u>

Trigonometric functions are periodic. Both sine and cosine have period 2π. For each input angle value, the output value follows around the unit circle. Once it reaches the starting point, it continues around and around the circle. It is true that $\sin(0) = \sin(2\pi) = \sin(4\pi)$, etc., and $\cos(0) = \cos(2\pi) = \cos(4\pi)$. Tangent has period π, and its output values repeat themselves every half of the unit circle. The domain of sine and cosine are all real numbers, and the domain of tangent is all real numbers, except the points where cosine equals zero. It is also true that $\sin(-x) = -\sin x$, $\cos(-x) = \cos(x)$, and $\tan(-x) = -\tan(x)$, so sine and tangent are odd functions, while cosine is an even function. Sine and tangent are symmetric with respect the origin, and cosine is symmetric with respect to the y-axis.

The graph of trigonometric functions can be used to model different situations. General forms are $y = a \sin b(x - h) + k$, and $y = a \cos b\,(x - h) + k$. The variable a represents the amplitude, which shows the maximum and minimum value of the function. The b is used to find the period by using the ratio $\frac{2\pi}{b}$, h is the horizontal shift, and k is the vertical shift. The equation $y = \sin(x)$ is shown on the following graph with the thick black line. The stretched graph of $y = 2\sin(x)$ is shown in solid black, and the shrunken graph $y = \frac{1}{2}\sin(x)$ is shown with the dotted line.

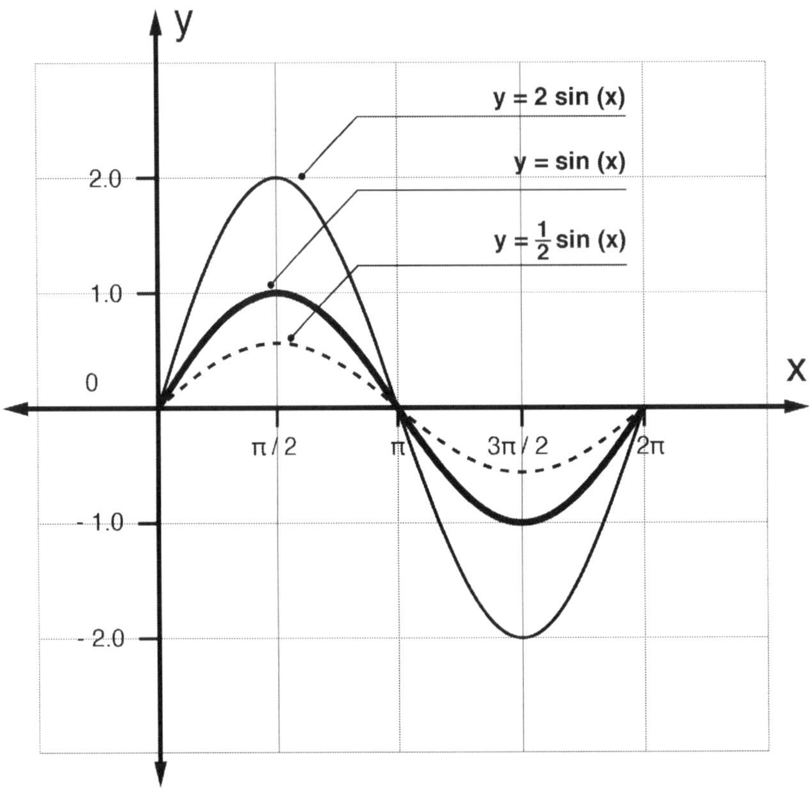

Trigonometric functions are used to find unknown ratios for a given angle measure. The inverse of these trig functions is used to find the unknown angle, given a ratio. For example, the expression $\arcsin(\frac{1}{2})$ means finding the value of x for $\sin(x) = \frac{1}{2}$. Since $\sin(\theta) = \frac{y}{1}$ on the unit circle, the angle whose y-value is $\frac{1}{2}$ is $\frac{\pi}{6}$. The inverse of any of the trigonometric functions can be used to find a missing angle measurement. Values not found on the unit circle can be found using the trigonometric functions on the calculator, making sure its mode is set to degrees or radians.

In order for the inverse to exist, the function must be one-to-one over its domain. There cannot be two input values connected to the same output. For example, the following graphs show the functions $y = \cos(x)$ and $y = \arccos(x)$. In order to have an inverse, the domain of cosine is restricted from 0 to π. Therefore, the range of its inverse function is $[0, \pi]$.

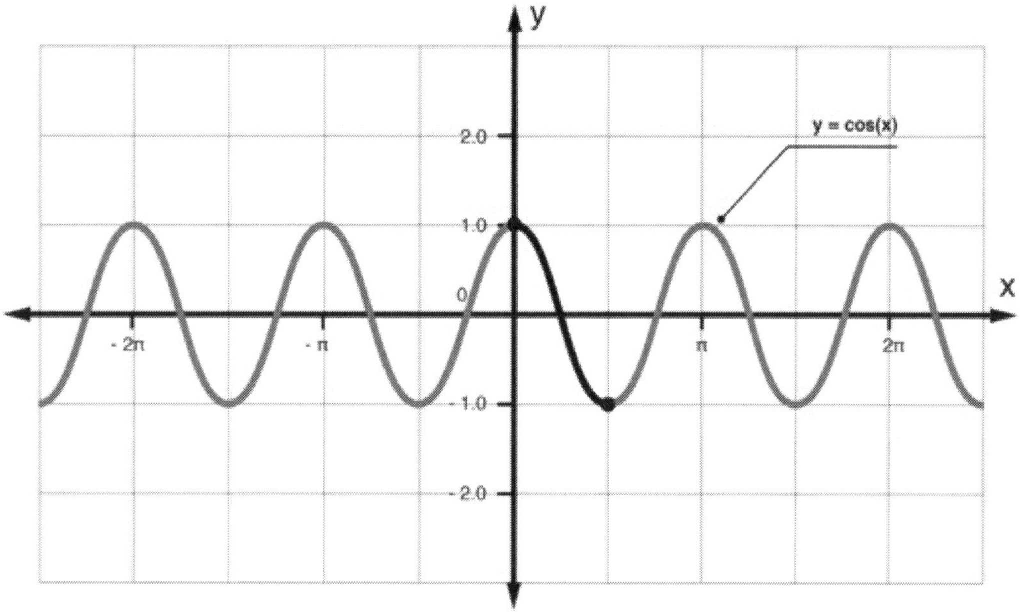

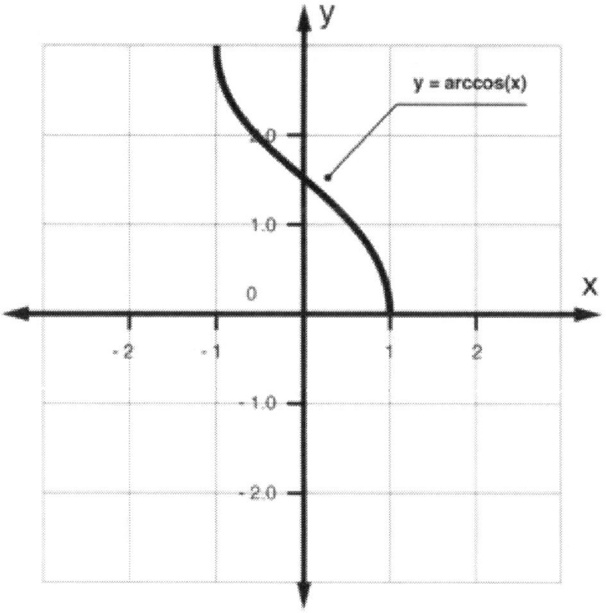

Inverses of trigonometric functions can be used to solve real-world problems. For example, there are many situations where the lengths of a perceived triangle can be found, but the angles are unknown. Consider a problem where the height of a flag (25 feet) and the distance on the ground to the flag is given (42 feet). The unknown, x, is the angle. To find this angle, the equation $\tan x = \frac{42}{25}$ is used. To solve for x, the inverse function can be used to turn the equation into $\tan^{-1}\frac{42}{25} = x$. Using the calculator, in degree mode, the answer is found to be $x = 59.2$ degrees

Trigonometric Identities

From the unit circle, the trigonometric ratios were found for the special right triangle with a hypotenuse of 1.

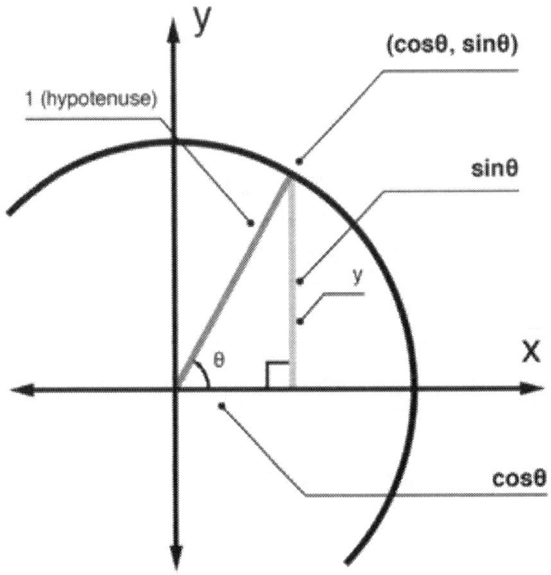

From this triangle, the following Pythagorean identities are formed: $\sin^2\theta + \cos^2\theta = 1$, $\tan^2\theta + 1 = \sec^2\theta$, and $1 + \cot^2\theta = \csc^2\theta$. The second two identities are formed by manipulating the first identity. Since identities are statements that are true for any value of the variable, then they may be used to manipulate equations. For example, a problem may ask for simplification of the expression $\cos^2 x + \cos^2 x\tan^2 x$. Using the fact that $\tan(x) = \frac{\sin x}{\cos x}$, $\frac{\sin^2 x}{\cos^2 x}$ can then be substituted in for $\tan^2 x$, making the expression:

$$\cos^2 x + \cos^2 x\frac{\sin^2 x}{\cos^2 x}$$

Then the two $\cos^2 x$ terms on top and bottom cancel each other out, simplifying the expression to $\cos^2 x + \sin^2 x$. By the first Pythagorean identity stated above, the expression can be turned into $\cos^2 x + \sin^2 x = 1$.

Another set of trigonometric identities are the double-angle formulas:

$$\sin 2\alpha = 2 \sin \alpha \ \cos \alpha$$

$$\cos 2\alpha = \begin{cases} \cos^2\alpha - \sin^2\alpha \\ 2 \cos^2\alpha - 1 \\ 1 - 2 \sin^2\alpha \end{cases}$$

Using these formulas, the following identity can be proved:

$$\sin 2x = \frac{2 \tan x}{1 + \tan^2 x}$$

By using one of the Pythagorean identities, the denominator can be rewritten as $1 + \tan^2 x = \sec^2 x$. By knowing the reciprocals of the trigonometric identities, the secant term can be rewritten to form the equation:

$$\sin 2x = \frac{2 \tan x}{1} * \cos^2 x$$

Replacing $\tan(x)$, the equation becomes $\sin 2x = \frac{2 \sin x}{\cos} * \cos^2 x$, where the $\cos x$ can cancel out. The new equation is $\sin 2x = 2 \sin x * \cos x$. This final equation is one of the double-angle formulas.

Other trigonometric identities such as half-angle formulas, sum and difference formulas, and difference of angles formulas can be used to prove and rewrite trigonometric equations. Depending on the given equation or expression, the correct identities need to be chosen to write equivalent statements.

The graph of sine is equal to the graph of cosine, shifted $\frac{\pi}{2}$ units. Therefore, the function $y = \sin x$ is equal to $y = \cos(\frac{\pi}{2} - x)$. Within functions, adding a constant to the independent variable shifts the graph either left or right. By shifting the cosine graph, the curve lies on top of the sine function. By transforming the function, the two equations give the same output for any given input.

Solving Trigonometric Functions

Solving trigonometric functions can be done with a knowledge of the unit circle and the trigonometric identities. It requires the use of opposite operations combined with trigonometric ratios for special triangles. For example, the problem may require solving the equation $2 \cos^2 x - \sqrt{3} \cos x = 0$ for the values of x between 0 and 180 degrees. The first step is to factor out the $\cos x$ term, resulting in $\cos x\,(2 \cos x - \sqrt{3}) = 0$. By the factoring method of solving, each factor can be set equal to zero: $\cos x = 0$ and $(2 \cos x - \sqrt{3}) = 0$. The second equation can be solved to yield the following equation: $\cos x = \frac{\sqrt{3}}{2}$. Now that the value of x is found, the trigonometric ratios can be used to find the solutions of $x = 30$ and 90 degrees.

Solving trigonometric functions requires the use of algebra to isolate the variable and a knowledge of trigonometric ratios to find the value of the variable. The unit circle can be used to find answers for special triangles. Beyond those triangles, a calculator can be used to solve for variables within the trigonometric functions.

Using Graphing Calculators to Solve Trigonometric Problems

In addition to algebraic techniques, problems involving trigonometric functions can be solved using graphing calculators. For example, given an equation, both sides of the equals sign first need to be graphed as separate equations in the same window on the calculator. The point(s) of intersection are then found by zooming into an appropriate window. The points of intersection are the solutions. For example, consider $\cos x = \frac{1}{2}$. Solving this equation involves graphing both $y = \cos x$ and $y = \frac{1}{2}$ in the same window. If the calculator is set in Radians mode, the screen zoomed in from $[0, 2\pi]$ on the x-axis would look like:

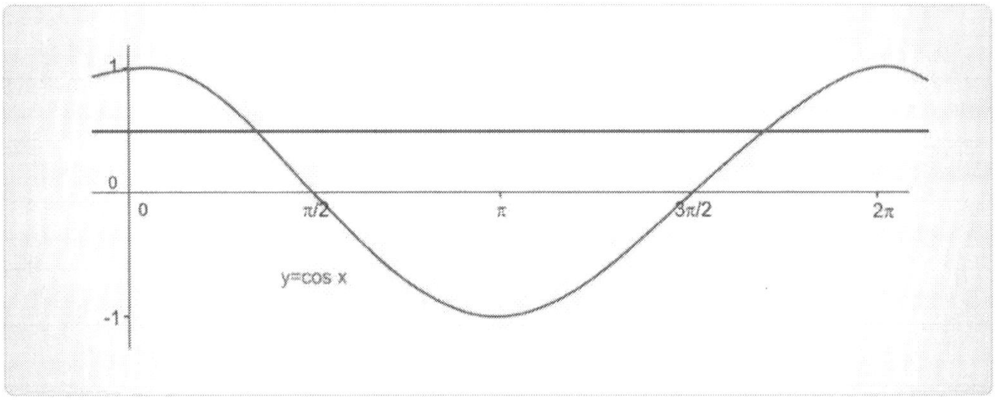

The trace function on the calculator allows the user to zoom into the point of intersection to obtain the two solutions from $[0, 2\pi]$. The periodic nature of the function must then be taken into consideration to obtain the entire solution set, which contains an infinite number of solutions.

Practice Questions

1. What is the volume of a cube with the side equal to 3 inches?
   a. 6 in^3
   b. 27 in^3
   c. 9 in^3
   d. 3 in^3
   e. 81 in^3

2. What is the volume of a cube with the side equal to 5 centimeters?
   a. 10 cm^3
   b. 15 cm^3
   c. 50 cm^3
   d. 25 cm^3
   e. 125 cm^3

3. What is the volume of a rectangular prism with a height of 2 inches, a width of 4 inches, and a depth of 6 inches?
   a. 12 in^3
   b. 24 in^3
   c. 48 in^3
   d. 60 in^3
   e. 96 in^3

4. What is the volume of a rectangular prism with the height of 3 centimeters, a width of 5 centimeters, and a depth of 11 centimeters?
   a. 19 cm^3
   b. 165 cm^3
   c. 225 cm^3
   d. 150 cm^3
   e. 88 cm^3

5. What is the volume of a pyramid, with the area of the base measuring 12 $inches^2$, and the height measuring 15 inches?
   a. 180 in^3
   b. 90 in^3
   c. 30 in^3
   d. 60 in^3
   e. 45 in^3

6. A pizzeria owner regularly creates jumbo pizzas, each with a radius of 9 inches. She is mathematically inclined, and wants to know the area of the pizza to purchase the correct boxes and know how much she is feeding her customers. What is the area of the circle, in terms of π, with a radius of 9 inches?
   a. 3 π in^2
   b. 18 π in^2
   c. 90 π in^2
   d. 9 π in^2
   e. 81 π in^2

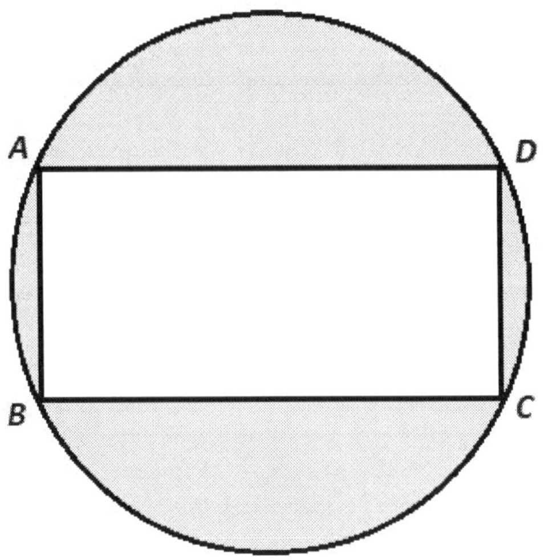

7. Rectangle *ABCD* is inscribed in the circle above. The length of side *AB* is 9 inches and the length of side *BC* is 12 inches. What is the area of the shaded region?

a. 64.4 sq. in.
b. 68.6 sq. in.
c. 62.8 sq. in.
d. 61.3 sq. in.
e. 64.6 sq. in.

8. For the following similar triangles, what are the values of x and y (rounded to one decimal place)?

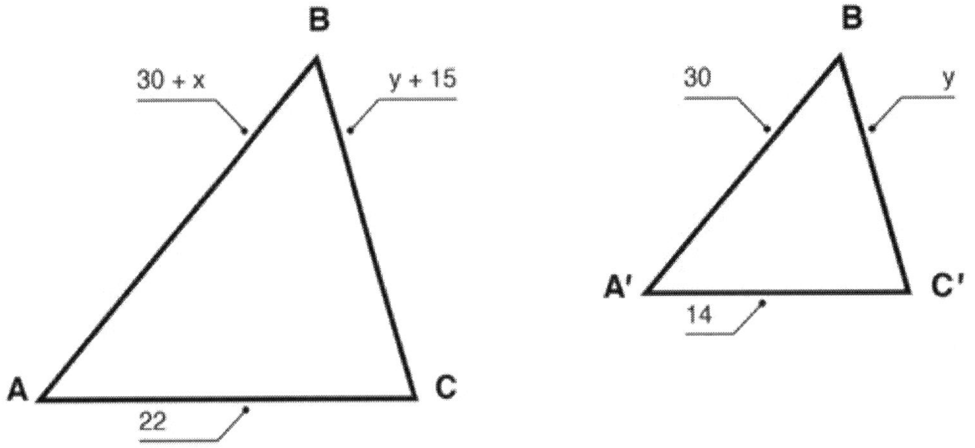

a. $x = 16.5, y = 25.1$
b. $x = 19.5, y = 24.1$
c. $x = 17.1, y = 26.3$
d. $x = 26.3, y = 17.1$
e. $x = 24.1, y = 19.5$

9. If the volume of a sphere is 288π cubic meters, what are the radius and surface area of the same sphere?

a. Radius 6 meters and surface area 144π square meters
b. Radius 36 meters and surface area 144π square meters
c. Radius 6 meters and surface area 12π square meters
d. Radius 36 meters and surface area 12π square meters
e. Radius 12 meters and surface area 144π square meters

10. The triangle shown below is a right triangle. What's the value of x?

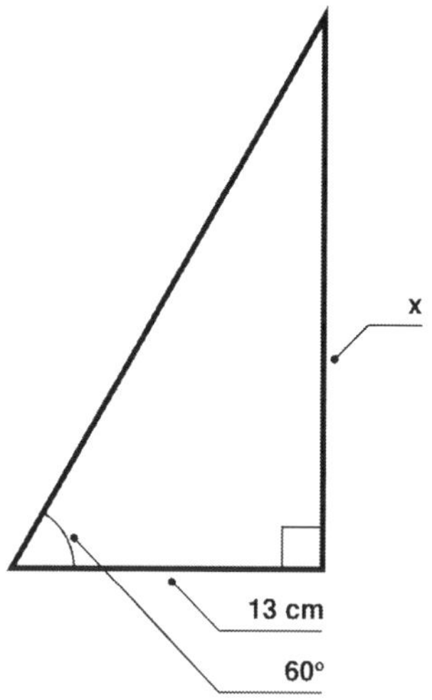

a. $x = 1.73$
b. $x = 0.57$
c. $x = 13$
d. $x = 14.73$
e. $x = 22.49$

11. Using the following diagram, calculate the total circumference, rounding to the nearest decimal place:

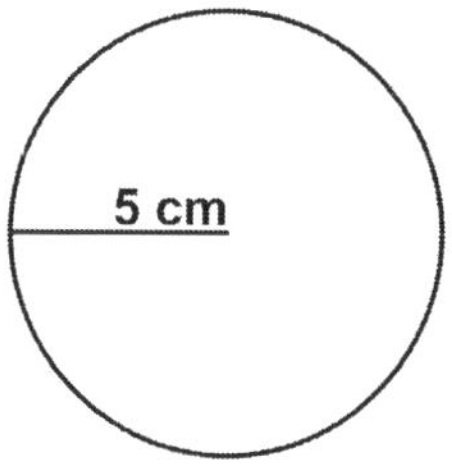

a. 25.0 cm
b. 15.7 cm
c. 78.5 cm
d. 50.0 cm
e. 31.4 cm

12. An angle measures 54 degrees. In order to correctly determine the measure of its complementary angle, what concept is necessary?

a. Two complementary angles sum up to 180 degrees.
b. Complementary angles are always acute.
c. Two complementary angles sum up to 90 degrees.
d. Complementary angles sum up to 360 degrees.
e. At least one of the angles of two complementary angles must be obtuse.

13. A triangular pyramid is composed of all equilateral triangles with sides measuring 8 cm. What is the surface area of the pyramid?

a. 128 sq. cm.
b. 110.7 sq. cm.
c. 114.6 sq. cm.
d. 117.8 sq. cm.
e. 27.68 sq. cm.

14. What are the center and radius of a circle with equation $4x^2 + 4y^2 - 16x - 24y + 51 = 0$?

a. Center (3, 2) and radius ½
b. Center (2, 3) and radius ½
c. Center (3, 2) and radius ¼
d. Center (2, 3) and radius ¼
e. Center (2, 2) and radius ¼

15. If the ordered pair $(-3, -4)$ is reflected over the *x*-axis, what's the new ordered pair?

a. $(-3, -4)$
b. $(3, -4)$
c. $(3, 4)$
d. $(-3, 4)$
e. $(-4, -3)$

16. What's the midpoint of a line segment with endpoints $(-1, 2)$ and $(3, -6)$?

a. $(1, 2)$
b. $(1, 0)$
c. $(-1, 2)$
d. $(1, -2)$
e. $(1, 4)$

17. Given the following triangle, what's the length of the missing side? Round the answer to the nearest tenth.

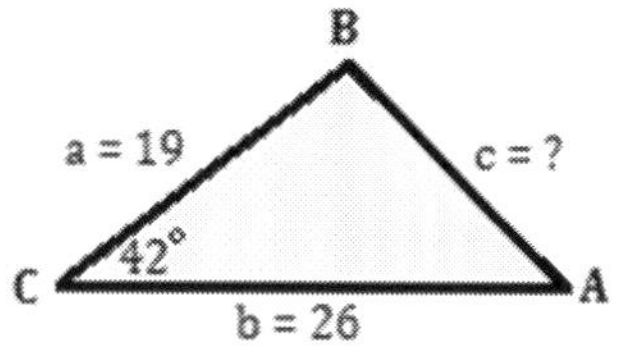

a. 17.0
b. 17.4
c. 18.0
d. 18.4
e. 17.2

18. What are the coordinates of the focus of the parabola $y = -9x^2$?
a. $(-3, 0)$
b. $\left(-\frac{1}{36}, 0\right)$
c. $(0, -3)$
d. $\left(-3, -\frac{1}{36}\right)$
e. $\left(0, -\frac{1}{36}\right)$

19. According to building code regulations, the roof of a house has to be set at a minimum angle of 39° up to a maximum angle of 48° to ensure snow and rain will properly slide off it. What is the maximum incline in terms of radians?
a. $\frac{\pi}{4}$
b. $\frac{\pi}{15}$
c. $\frac{4\pi}{15}$
d. $\frac{3\pi}{4}$
e. $\frac{48}{90}$

20. An arc is intercepted by a central angle of 240°. What is the number of radians of that angle?
a. $\frac{3\pi}{4}$
b. $\frac{4\pi}{3}$
c. $\frac{\pi}{4}$
d. $\frac{\pi}{3}$
e. $\frac{3}{4\pi}$

Answer Explanations

1. B: The volume of a cube is the length of the side cubed, and 3 inches cubed is 27 in^3. Choice *A* is not the correct answer because that is 2×3 inches. Choice *C* is not the correct answer because that is 3×3 inches, and Choice *D* is not the correct answer because there was no operation performed. Choice *E* in incorrect because that is $3 \times 3 \times 3 \times 3$ inches.

2. E: The volume of a cube is the length of the side cubed, and 5 centimeters cubed is 125 cm^3. Choice *A* is not the correct answer because that is 2×5 centimeters. Choice *B* is not the correct answer because that is 3×5 centimeters. Choice *C* is not the correct answer because that is 5×10 centimeters and Choice *D* is not correct because that is 5×5 inches.

3. C: The volume of a rectangular prism is $length \times width \times height$, and $2\ inches \times 4\ inches \times 6\ inches\ is\ 48\ in^3$. Choice *A* is not the correct answer because that is $2\ inches \times 6\ inches$. Choice *B* is not the correct answer because that is $4\ inches \times 6\ inches$. Choice *D* is not correct because the answer reflects calculation errors and Choice *E* is not the correct answer because it is double of all the sides multiplied together.

4. B: The volume of a rectangular prism is the $length \times width \times height$, and $3cm \times 5cm \times 11cm$ is 165 cm^3. Choice *A* is not the correct answer because that is $3cm + 5cm + 11cm$. Choice *C* is not the correct answer because that is 15^2. Choice *D* is not the correct answer because that is $3cm \times 5cm \times 10cm$. Lastly, Choice *E* is incorrect because it is $(3cm + 5cm) \times 11cm$.

5. D: The volume of a pyramid is ($length \times width \times height$), divided by 3, and (12×15), divided by 3 is 60 in^3. Choice *A* is not the correct answer because that is 12×15. Choice *B* is not the correct answer because that is (12×15), divided by 2. Choice *C* is not the correct answer because that is 15×2. Choice *E* is not the correct answer because that is (12×15), divided by 4.

6. E: The formula for the area of the circle is πr^2 and 9 squared is 81. Choice *A* is not the correct answer because that takes the square root of the radius instead of squaring the radius. Choice *B* is not the correct answer because that is 2×9. Choice *C* is not the correct answer because that is 9×10. Choice *D* is not the correct answer because that is simply the value of the radius.

7. B: The inscribed rectangle is 9 X 12 inches. First find the length of *AC* using the Pythagorean Theorem. So, $9^2 + 12^2 = c^2$, where *c* is the length of *AC* in this case. This means that *AC* = 15 inches. This means the diameter of the circle is 15 inches. This can be used to find the area of the entire circle. The formula is πr^2. So, $3.14(7.5)^2 = 176.6$ sq. inches. Then take the area of the rectangle away to find just the area of the shaded region. This is 176.6 – 108 = 68.6.

8. C: Because the triangles are similar, the lengths of the corresponding sides are proportional. Therefore:

$$\frac{30 + x}{30} = \frac{22}{14} = \frac{y + 15}{y}$$

This results in the equation $14(30 + x) = 22 \cdot 30$ which, when solved, gives $x = 17.1$. The proportion also results in the equation $14(y + 15) = 22y$ which, when solved, gives $y = 26.3$.

9. A: Because the volume of the given sphere is 288π cubic meters, this means ${}^{4}/{}_{3}\,\pi r^3 = 288\pi$. This equation is solved for r to obtain a radius of 6 meters. The formula for the surface area of a sphere is $4\pi r^2$, so if $r = 6$ in this formula, the surface area is 144π square meters.**10. E:** SOHCAHTOA is used to find the missing side length. Because the angle and adjacent side are known, $\tan 60 = \frac{x}{13}$. Making sure to evaluate tangent with an argument in degrees, this equation gives $x = 13 \tan 60 = 13 \cdot 1.73 = 22.49$.

11. E: To calculate the circumference of a circle, use the formula $2\pi r$, where r equals the radius or half of the diameter of the circle and $\pi = 3.14 \dots$. Substitute the given information, $2\pi 5 = 31.4 \dots$, answer *E*.

12. C: The measure of two complementary angles sums up to 90 degrees. $90 - 54 = 36$. Therefore, the complementary angle is 36 degrees.

13. B: To solve this, first find the area of one of the sides. Then multiply times 4 since all sides are identical. To find the area of a side use the formula $\frac{1}{2}bh$, where *b* is the base and *h* is the height of the triangle. For this it is given that the base is 8 cm. To calculate the height, use the Pythagorean Theorem. So, make a smaller triangle within this one where the height will be the unknown side. So, $4^2 + b^2 = 8^2$, $64 - 16 = 48$, $\sqrt{48} = 6.92$. The height of this triangle is 6.92 cm. Now plug this into the formula for area. So, $\frac{1}{2}(8)(6.92) = 27.68$. Then multiply times 4 to get 110.7 as the total surface area.

14. B: The technique of completing the square must be used to change $4x^2 + 4y^2 - 16x - 24y + 51 = 0$ into the standard equation of a circle. First, the constant must be moved to the right-hand side of the equals sign, and each term must be divided by the coefficient of the x^2 term (which is 4). The x and y terms must be grouped together to obtain:

$$x^2 - 4x + y^2 - 6y = -\frac{51}{4}$$

Then, the process of completing the square must be completed for each variable. This gives:

$$(x^2 - 4x + 4) + (y^2 - 6y + 9) = -\frac{51}{4} + 4 + 9$$

The equation can be written as:

$$(x - 2)^2 + (y - 3)^2 = \frac{1}{4}$$

Therefore, the center of the circle is (2, 3) and the radius is:

$$\sqrt{\frac{1}{4}} = \frac{1}{2}$$

15. D: When an ordered pair is reflected over an axis, the sign of one of the coordinates must change. When it's reflected over the x-axis, the sign of the x coordinate must change. The *y* value remains the same. Therefore, the new ordered pair is $(-3, 4)$.

16. D: The midpoint formula should be used.

$$M = \left(\frac{x_1 + x_2}{2}, \frac{y_1 + y_2}{2}\right) = \left(\frac{-1+3}{2}, \frac{2+(-6)}{2}\right) = (1, -2)$$

17. B: Because this isn't a right triangle, SOHCAHTOA can't be used. However, the law of cosines can be used. Therefore:

$$c^2 = a^2 + b^2 - 2ab\ \cos C = 19^2 + 26^2 - 2 \cdot 19 \cdot 26 \cdot \cos 42° = 302.773$$

Taking the square root and rounding to the nearest tenth results in $c = 17.4$.

18. E: A parabola of the form $y = \frac{1}{4f}x^2$ has a focus $(0, f)$. Because $y = -9x^2$, set $-9 = \frac{1}{4f}$. Solving this equation for f results in $f = -\frac{1}{36}$. Therefore, the coordinates of the focus are $\left(0, -\frac{1}{36}\right)$.

19. C: When you simplify $\frac{48° \times \pi}{180}$, you get $\frac{4\pi}{15}$. Choice *A* is not the correct answer because $\frac{\pi}{4}$ is 45°. Choice *B* is not the correct answer because $\frac{\pi}{15}$ is 12°. Choice *D* is not the correct answer because $\frac{3\pi}{4} = 135°$. Choice *E* is not the correct answer because the initial equation was set the incorrect denominator (90 instead of 180) and failed to simplify.

20. B: When you simplify $(\frac{4\pi}{3}) \times (\frac{\pi}{180})$, you get $\frac{4\pi}{3}$. Choice *A* is not the correct answer because it is the reciprocal of $\frac{4\pi}{3}$. Choice *C* is not the correct answer because it is not the correct reduction of the fraction. Choice *D* is not the correct answer because it is not the correct reduction of the fraction. Choice *E* is incorrect because it is the reciprocal of the correct answer.

Data Analysis, Statistics, and Probability

Statistical Questions

A statistical question is answered by collecting data with variability. Data consists of facts and/or statistics (numbers), and variability refers to a tendency to shift or change. Data is a broad term, inclusive of things like height, favorite color, name, salary, temperature, gas mileage, and language. Questions requiring data as an answer are not necessarily statistical questions. If there is no variability in the data, then the question is not statistical in nature. Consider the following examples: what is Mary's favorite color? How much money does your mother make? What was the highest temperature last week? How many miles did your car get on its last tank of gas? How much taller than Bob is Ed?

None of the above are statistical questions because each case lacks variability in the data needed to answer the question. The questions on favorite color, salary, and gas mileage each require a single piece of data, whether a fact or statistic. Therefore, variability is absent. Although the temperature question requires multiple pieces of data (the high temperature for each day), a single, distinct number is the answer. The height question requires two pieces of data, Bob's height and Ed's height, but no difference in variability exists between those two values. Therefore, this is not a statistical question. Statistical questions typically require calculations with data.

Consider the following statistical questions:

How many miles per gallon of gas does the 2016 Honda Civic get? To answer this question, data must be collected. This data should include miles driven and gallons used. Different cars, different drivers, and different driving conditions will produce different results. Therefore, variability exists in the data. To answer the question, the mean (average) value could be determined.

Are American men taller than Chinese men? To answer this question, data must be collected. This data should include the heights of American men and the heights of Chinese men. All American men are not the same height and all Chinese men are not the same height. Some American men are taller than some Chinese men and some Chinese men are taller than some American men. Therefore, variability exists in the data. To answer the question, the median values for each group could be determined and compared.

The following are more examples of statistical questions: What proportion of 4th graders have a favorite color of blue? How much money do teachers make? Is it colder in Boston or Chicago?

Mean, Median, and Mode

<u>Mean</u>
Suppose that you have a set of data points and some description of the general properties of this data need to be found.

The first property that can be defined for this set of data is the *mean*. This is the same as average. To find the mean, add up all the data points, then divide by the total number of data points. For example, suppose that in a class of 10 students, the scores on a test were 50, 60, 65, 65, 75, 80, 85, 85, 90, 100. Therefore, the average test score will be:

$$\frac{50+60+65+65+75+80+85+85+90+100}{10}=75.5$$

The mean is a useful number if the distribution of data is normal (more on this later), which roughly means that the frequency of different outcomes has a single peak and is roughly equally distributed on both sides of that peak. However, it is less useful in some cases where the data might be split or where there are some *outliers*. Outliers are data points that are far from the rest of the data. For example, suppose there are 10 executives and 90 employees at a company. The executives make $1000 per hour, and the employees make $10 per hour.

Therefore, the average pay rate will be:

$$\frac{\$1000 \cdot 11 + \$10 \cdot 90}{100} = \$119\, per\ hour$$

In this case, this average is not very descriptive since it's not close to the actual pay of the executives *or* the employees.

Median

Another useful measurement is the *median*. In a data set, the median is the point in the middle. The middle refers to the point where half the data comes before it and half comes after, when the data is recorded in numerical order. For instance, these are the speeds of the fastball of a pitcher during the last inning that he pitched (in order from least to greatest):

90, 92, 93, 93, 95, 96, 97, 97, 97

There are nine total numbers, so the middle or *median* number in the 5th one, which is 95.

In cases where the number of data points is an even number, then the average of the two middle points is taken. In the previous example of test scores, the two middle points are 75 and 80. Since there is no single point, the average of these two scores needs to be found. The average is:

$$\frac{75 + 80}{2} = 77.5$$

The median is generally a good value to use if there are a few outliers in the data. It prevents those outliers from affecting the "middle" value as much as when using the mean.

Since an outlier is a data point that is far from most of the other data points in a data set, this means an outlier also is any point that is far from the median of the data set. The outliers can have a substantial effect on the mean of a data set, but usually do not change the median or mode, or do not change them by a large quantity. For example, consider the data set (3, 5, 6, 6, 6, 8). This has a median of 6 and a mode of 6, with a mean of $\frac{34}{6} \approx 5.67$. Now, suppose a new data point of 1000 is added so that the data set is now (3, 5, 6, 6, 6, 8, 1000). This does not change the median or mode, which are both still 6. However, the average is now $\frac{1034}{7}$, which is approximately 147.7. In this case, the median and mode will be better descriptions for most of the data points.

The reason for outliers in a given data set is a complicated problem. It is sometimes the result of an error by the experimenter, but often they are perfectly valid data points that must be taken into consideration.

Mode

One additional measure to define for *X* is the *mode*. This is the data point that appears most frequently. If two or more data points all tie for the most frequent appearance, then each of them is considered a mode. In the case of the test scores, where the numbers were 50, 60, 65, 65, 75, 80, 85, 85, 90, 100, there are two modes: 65 and 85.

Quartiles and Percentiles

The *first quartile* of a set of data *X* refers to the largest value from the first ¼ of the data points. In practice, there are sometimes slightly different definitions that can be used, such as the median of the first half of the data points (excluding the median itself if there are an odd number of data points). The term also has a slightly different use: when it is said that a data point lies *in the first quartile*, it means it is less than or equal to the median of the first half of the data points. Conversely, if it lies *at* the first quartile, then it is equal to the first quartile.

When it is said that a data point lies in the *second quartile*, it means it is between the first quartile and the median.

The *third quartile* refers to data that lies between ½ and ¾ of the way through the data set. Again, there are various methods for defining this precisely, but the simplest way is to include all of the data that lie between the median and the median of the top half of the data.

Data that lies in the *fourth quartile* refers to all of the data above the third quartile.

Percentiles may be defined in a similar manner to quartiles. Generally, this is defined in the following manner:

If a data point lies *in the n-th percentile*, this means it lies in the range of the first *n*% of the data.

If a data point lies *at* the *n*-th percentile, then it means that *n*% of the data lies below this data point.

Standard Deviation

Given a data set *X* consisting of data points $(x_1, x_2, x_3, \dots x_n)$, the *variance* of *X* is defined to be:

$$\frac{\sum_{i=1}^{n}(x_i - \bar{X})^2}{n}$$

This means that the variance of *X* is the average of the squares of the differences between each data point and the mean of *X*.

Given a data set *X* consisting of data points $(x_1, x_2, x_3, \dots x_n)$, the *standard deviation* of *X* is defined to be:

$$s_x = \sqrt{\frac{\sum_{i=1}^{n}(x_i - \bar{X})^2}{n}}$$

In other words, the standard deviation is the square root of the variance.

Both the variance and the standard deviation are measures of how much the data tend to be spread out. When the standard deviation is low, the data points are mostly clustered around the mean. When the standard deviation is high, this generally indicates that the data are quite spread out, or else that there are a few substantial outliers.

As a simple example, compute the standard deviation for the data set (1, 3, 3, 5). First, compute the mean, which will be $\frac{1+3+3+5}{4} = \frac{12}{4} = 3$. Now, find the variance of X with the formula:

$$\sum_{i=1}^{4}(x_i - \bar{X})^2 = (1-3)^2 + (3-3)^2 + (5-3)^2 = -2^2 + 0^2 + 0^2 + 2^2 = 8$$

Therefore, the variance is $\frac{8}{4} = 2$. Taking the square root, the standard deviation will be $\sqrt{2}$.

Note that the standard deviation only depends upon the mean, not upon the median or mode(s). Generally, if there are multiple modes that are far apart from one another, the standard deviation will be high. A high standard deviation does not always mean there are multiple modes, however.

Best Description of a Set of Data

Measures of central tendency, namely mean, median, and mode, describe characteristics of a set of data. Specifically, they are intended to represent a *typical* value in the set by identifying a central position of the set. Depending on the characteristics of a specific set of data, different measures of central tendency are more indicative of a typical value in the set.

When a data set is grouped closely together with a relatively small range and the data is spread out somewhat evenly, the mean is an effective indicator of a typical value in the set. Consider the following data set representing the height of sixth grade boys in inches: 61 inches, 54 inches, 58 inches, 63 inches, 58 inches. The mean of the set is 58.8 inches. The data set is grouped closely (the range is only 9 inches) and the values are spread relatively evenly (three values below the mean and two values above the mean). Therefore, the mean value of 58.8 inches is an effective measure of central tendency in this case.

When a data set contains a small number of values either extremely large or extremely small when compared to the other values, the mean is not an effective measure of central tendency. Consider the following data set representing annual incomes of homeowners on a given street: $71,000; $74,000; $75,000; $77,000; $340,000. The mean of this set is $127,400. This figure does not indicate a typical value in the set, which contains four out of five values between $71,000 and $77,000. The median is a much more effective measure of central tendency for data sets such as these. Finding the middle value diminishes the influence of outliers, or numbers that may appear out of place, like the $340,000 annual income. The median for this set is $75,000 which is much more typical of a value in the set.

The mode of a data set is a useful measure of central tendency for categorical data when each piece of data is an option from a category. Consider a survey of 31 commuters asking how they get to work with results summarized below.

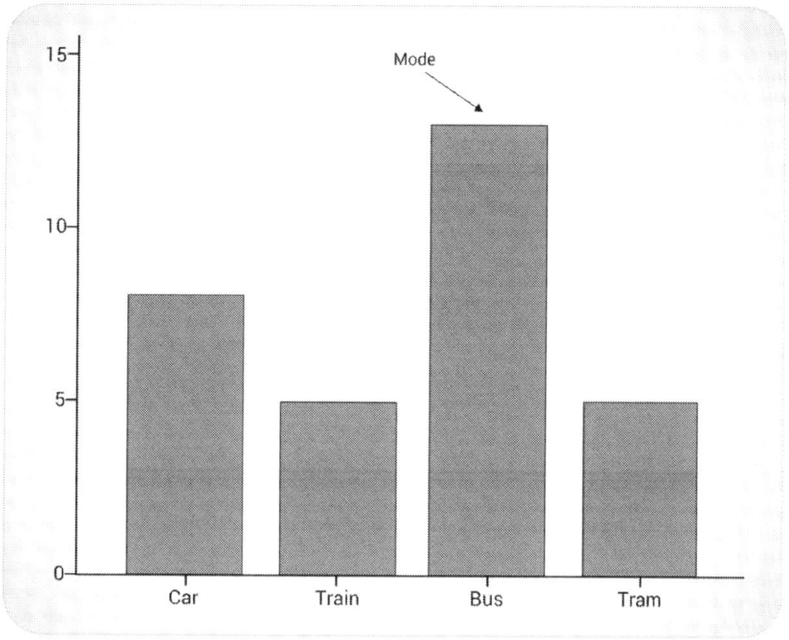

The mode for this set represents the value, or option, of the data that repeats most often. This indicates that the bus is the most popular method of transportation for the commuters.

<u>Effects of Changes in Data</u>
Changing all values of a data set in a consistent way produces predictable changes in the measures of the center and range of the set. A linear transformation changes the original value into the new value by either adding a given number to each value, multiplying each value by a given number, or both. Adding (or subtracting) a given value to each data point will increase (or decrease) the mean, median, and any modes by the same value. However, the range will remain the same due to the way that range is calculated. Multiplying (or dividing) a given value by each data point will increase (or decrease) the mean, median, and any modes, and the range by the same factor.

Consider the following data set, call it set *P*, representing the price of different cases of soda at a grocery store: \$4.25, \$4.40, \$4.75, \$4.95, \$4.95, \$5.15. The mean of set *P* is \$4.74. The median is \$4.85. The mode of the set is \$4.95. The range is \$0.90. Suppose the state passes a new tax of \$0.25 on every case of soda sold. The new data set, set *T*, is calculated by adding \$0.25 to each data point from set *P*. Therefore, set *T* consists of the following values: \$4.50, \$4.65, \$5.00, \$5.20, \$5.20, \$5.40. The mean of set *T* is \$4.99. The median is \$5.10. The mode of the set is \$5.20. The range is \$.90. The mean, median and mode of set *T* is equal to \$0.25 added to the mean, median, and mode of set *P*. The range stays the same.

Now suppose, due to inflation, the store raises the cost of every item by 10 percent. Raising costs by 10 percent is calculated by multiplying each value by 1.1. The new data set, set *I*, is calculated by multiplying each data point from set *T* by 1.1. Therefore, set *I* consists of the following values: \$4.95, \$5.12, \$5.50, \$5.72, \$5.72, \$5.94. The mean of set *I* is \$5.49. The median is \$5.61. The mode of the set is

\$5.72. The range is \$0.99. The mean, median, mode, and range of set *I* is equal to 1.1 multiplied by the mean, median, mode, and range of set *T* because each increased by a factor of 10 percent.

Comparing Data

Data sets can be compared by looking at the center and spread of each set. Measures of central tendency involve median, mean, midrange, and mode. The *mode* of a data set is the data value or values that appears the most frequently. The *midrange* is equal to the maximum value plus the minimum value divided by two. The *median* is the value that is halfway into each data set; it splits the data into two intervals. The *mean* is the sum of all data values divided by the number of data points. Two completely different sets of data can have the same mean. For example, a data set having values ranging from 0 to 100 and a data set having values ranging from 44 to 46 could both have means equal to 50. The first data set would have a much wider range, which is known as the *spread* of the data. It measures how varied the data is within each set. Spread can be defined further as either interquartile range or standard deviation. The *interquartile range (IQR)* is the range of the middle fifty percent of the data set. The *standard deviation, s,* quantifies the amount of variation with respect to the mean. A lower standard deviation shows that the data set does not differ much from the mean. A larger standard deviation shows that the data set is spread out farther away from the mean. The formula for standard deviation is $s = \sqrt{\frac{\Sigma(x-\bar{x})^2}{n-1}}$, where x is each value in the data set, $\bar{x}$ is the mean, and n is the total number of data points in the sample set. The square of the standard deviation is known as the *variance* of the data set. A data set can have outliers, and measures of central tendency that are not affected by outliers are the mode and median. Those measures are labeled as resistant measures of center.

Describing a Set of Data

A set of data can be described in terms of its center, spread, shape and any unusual features. The center of a data set can be measured by its mean, median, or mode. The spread of a data set refers to how far the data points are from the center (mean or median). The spread can be measured by the range or the quartiles and interquartile range. A data set with data points clustered around the center will have a small spread. A data set covering a wide range will have a large spread.

When a data set is displayed as a histogram or frequency distribution plot, the shape indicates if a sample is normally distributed, symmetrical, or has measures of skewness or kurtosis. When graphed, a data set with a normal distribution will resemble a bell curve.

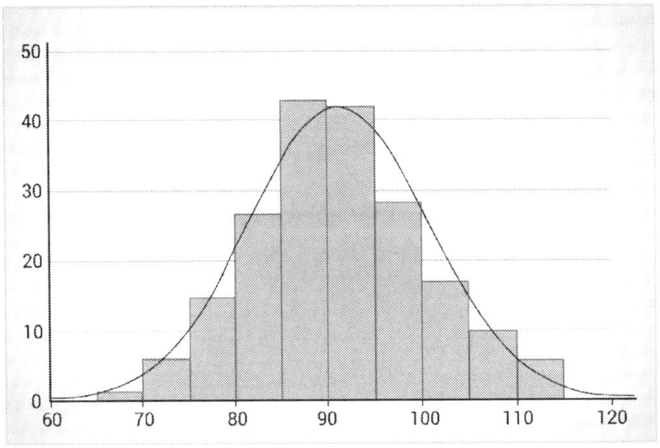

If the data set is symmetrical, each half of the graph when divided at the center is a mirror image of the other. If the graph has fewer data points to the right, the data is skewed right. If it has fewer data points to the left, the data is skewed left.

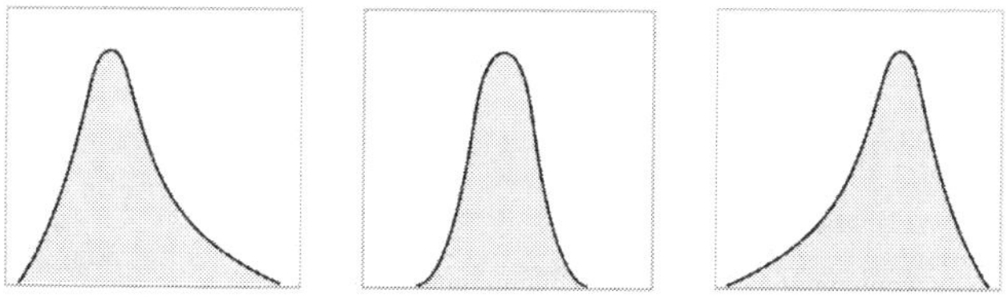

Right-Skewed Symmetric Left-Skewed

Kurtosis is a measure of whether the data is heavy-tailed with a high number of outliers, or light-tailed with a low number of outliers.

A description of a data set should include any unusual features such as gaps or outliers. A gap is a span within the range of the data set containing no data points. An outlier is a data point with a value either extremely large or extremely small when compared to the other values in the set.

<u>Normal Distribution</u>

A *normal distribution* of data follows the shape of a bell curve. In a normal distribution, the data set's median, mean, and mode are equal. Therefore, 50 percent of its values are less than the mean and 50 percent are greater than the mean. Data sets that follow this shape can be generalized using normal distributions. Normal distributions are described as *frequency distributions* in which the data set is plotted as percentages rather than true data points. A *relative frequency distribution* is one where the y-axis is between zero and 1, which is the same as 0% to 100%. Within a standard deviation, 68 percent of the values are within 1 standard deviation of the mean, 95 percent of the values are within 2 standard deviations of the mean, and 99.7 percent of the values are within 3 standard deviations of the mean. The number of standard deviations that a data point falls from the mean is called the *z-score*. The formula for the z-score is $Z = \frac{x-\mu}{\sigma}$, where μ is the mean, σ is the standard deviation, and x is the data point. This formula is used to fit any data set that resembles a normal distribution to a standard normal distribution, in a process known as *standardizing*.

Here is a normal distribution with labelled z-scores:

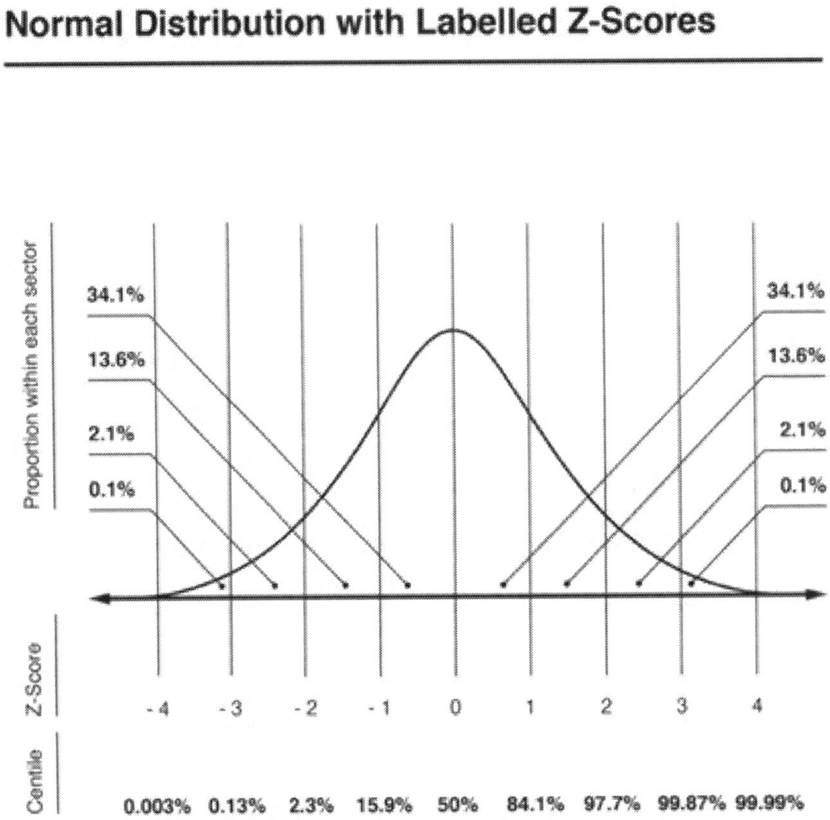

Population percentages can be estimated using normal distributions. For example, the probability that a data point will be less than the mean, or that the z-score will be less than 0, is 50%. Similarly, the probability that a data point will be within 1 standard deviation of the mean, or that the z-score will be between -1 and 1, is about 68.2%. When using a table, the left column states how many standard deviations (to one decimal place) away from the mean the point is, and the row heading states the second decimal place. The entries in the table corresponding to each column and row give the probability, which is equal to the area.

Creating and Interpreting Linear Regression Models

Linear Regression

Regression lines are a way to calculate a relationship between the independent variable and the dependent variable. A straight line means that there's a linear trend in the data. Technology can be used to find the equation of this line (e.g., a graphing calculator or Microsoft Excel®). In either case, all of the data points are entered, and a line is "fit" that best represents the shape of the data. Other functions used to model data sets include quadratic and exponential models.

Estimating Data Points

Regression lines can be used to estimate data points not already given. For example, if an equation of a line is found that fit the temperature and beach visitor data set, its input is the average daily temperature and its output is the projected number of visitors. Thus, the number of beach visitors on a 100-degree day can be estimated. The output is a data point on the regression line, and the number of daily visitors is expected to be greater than on a 96-degree day because the regression line has a positive slope.

Plotting and Analyzing Residuals

Once the function is found that fits the data, its accuracy can be calculated. Therefore, how well the line fits the data can be determined. The difference between the actual dependent variable from the data set and the estimated value located on the regression line is known as a ***residual*.** Therefore, the residual is known as the predicted value $\hat{y}$ minus the actual value y. A residual is calculated for each data point and can be plotted on the scatterplot. If all the residuals appear to be approximately the same distance from the regression line, the line is a good fit. If the residuals seem to differ greatly across the board, the line isn't a good fit.

Interpreting the Regression Line

The formula for a regression line is $y = mx + b$, where m is the slope and b is the *y*-intercept. Both the slope and *y*-intercept are found in the *Method of Least Squares*, which is the process of finding the equation of the line through minimizing residuals. The slope represents the rate of change in *y* as x gets larger. Therefore, because *y* is the dependent variable, the slope actually provides the predicted values given the independent variable. The *y*-intercept is the predicted value for when the independent variable equals zero. In the temperature example, the y-intercept is the expected number of beach visitors for a very cold average daily temperature of zero degrees.

Correlation Coefficient

The *correlation coefficient (r)* measures the association between two variables. Its value is between -1 and 1, where -1 represents a perfect negative linear relationship, 0 represents no relationship, and 1 represents a perfect positive linear relationship. A *negative linear relationship* means that as x values increase, *y* values decrease. A *positive linear relationship* means that as *x* values increase, *y* values increase. The formula for computing the correlation coefficient is:

$$r = \frac{n(\sum xy) - (\sum x)(\sum y)}{\sqrt{n(\sum x^2) - (\sum x)^2}\sqrt{n(\sum y^2) - (\Sigma y)^2}}$$

n is the number of data points

Both Microsoft Excel® and a graphing calculator can evaluate this easily once the data points are entered. A correlation greater than 0.8 or less than -0.8 is classified as "strong" while a correlation between -0.5 and 0.5 is classified as "weak."

Correlation Versus Causation

Correlation and causation have two different meanings. If two values are correlated, there is an association between them. However, correlation doesn't necessarily mean that one variable causes the other. *Causation* (or "cause and effect") occurs when one variable causes the other. Average daily temperature and number of beachgoers are correlated and have causation. If the temperature increases, the change in weather causes more people to go to the beach. However, alcoholism and smoking are correlated but don't have causation. The more someone drinks the more likely they are to smoke, but drinking alcohol doesn't cause someone to smoke.

Regression Models

Regression lines are straight lines that calculate a relationship between nonlinear data involving an independent variable and a dependent variable. A regression line is of the form $y = mx + b$, where

m is the slope and b is the y-intercept. Both the slope and y-intercept are found using the *Method of Least Squares*, which involves minimizing residuals – the difference between the dependent variable from the data set and the estimated value located on the regression line. The slope represents the rate of change in y as x increases. The y-intercept is the predicted value when the independent variable is equal to 0. Technology, such as a graphing calculator or Microsoft Excel®, can also be utilized to find the equation of this line. In either case, the data points are entered, and a line is "fit" that best represents the shape of the data. Here is an example of a data set and its regression line:

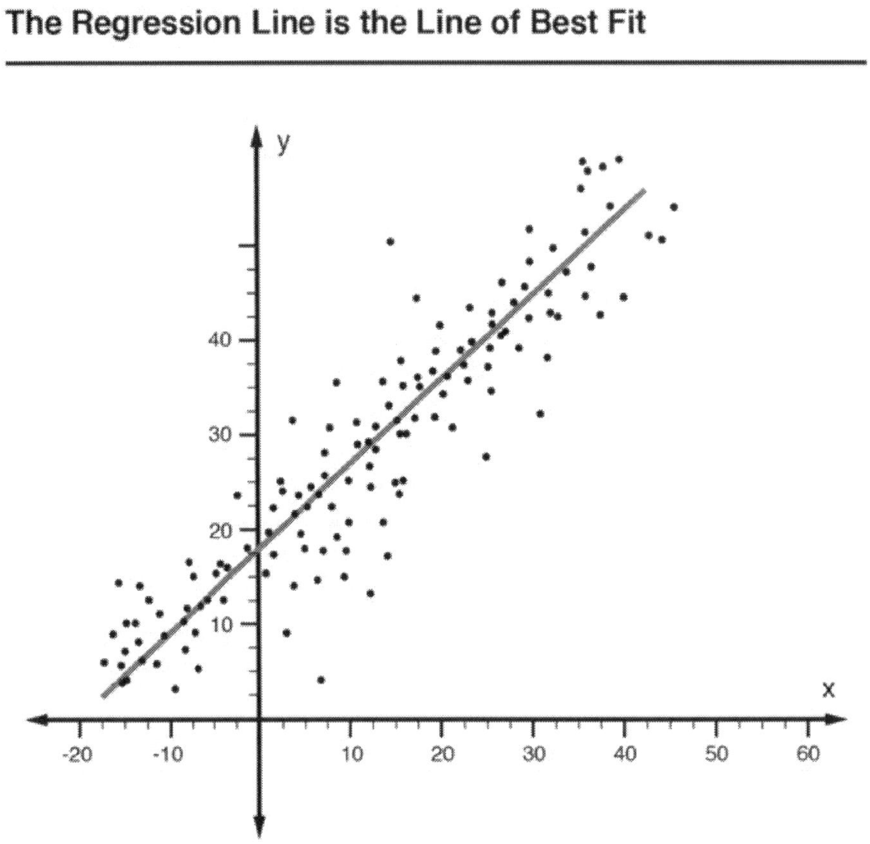

Regression models are highly used for forecasting, and linear regression techniques are the simplest models. If the nonlinear data follows the shape of exponential, logarithmic, or power functions, those types of functions can be used to more accurately model the data rather than lines.

Here is an example of both an exponential regression and a logarithmic regression model:

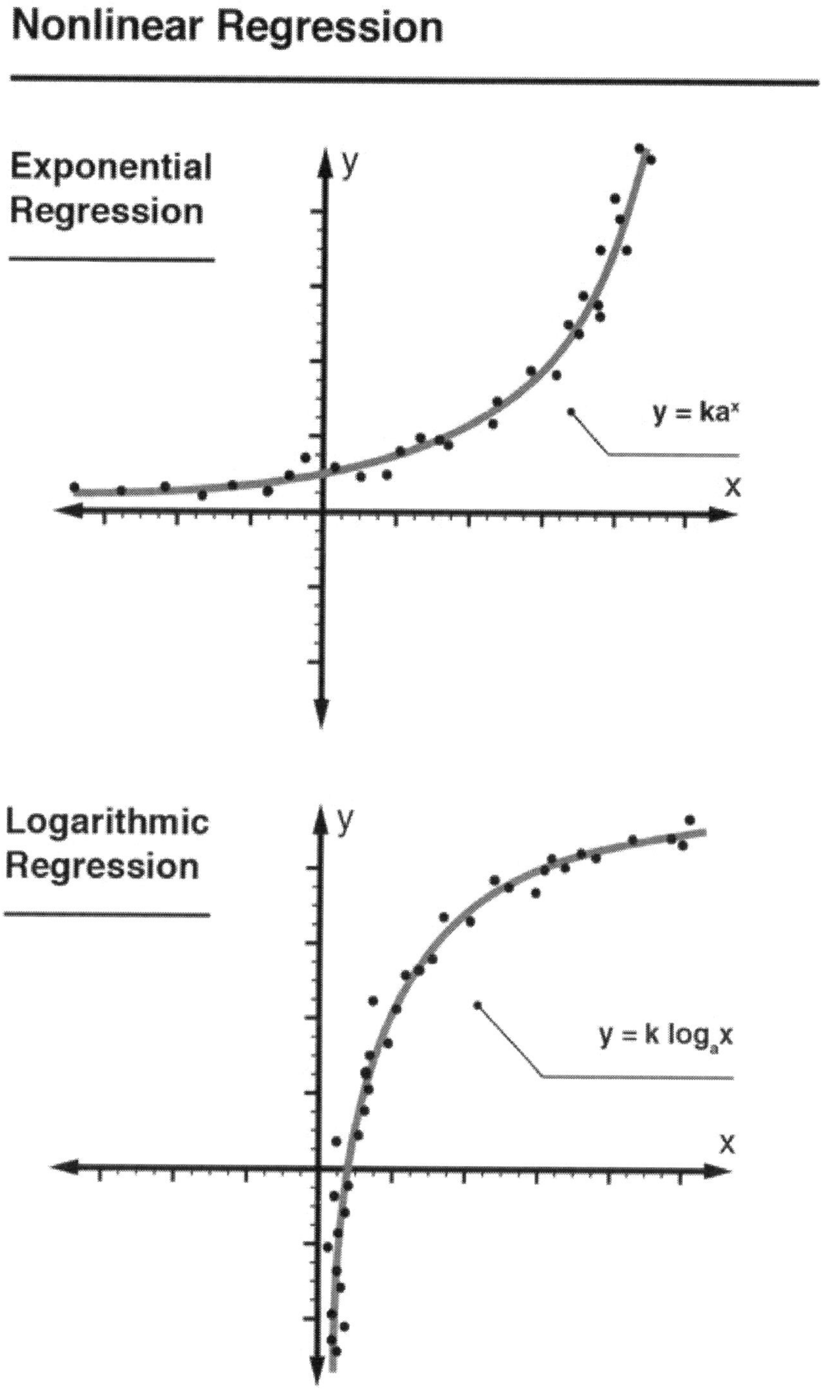

The Law of Large Numbers and the Central Limit Theorem

The *Law of Large Numbers* states that as the number of experiments increase, the actual ratio of outcomes will approach the theoretical probability. The *Central Limit Theorem* states that through using a sufficiently large sample size N, meaning over 30, the sampling distribution of the mean approaches a normal distribution with a mean of μ and variance of σ^2/N. The variance of the actual population is σ^2 and its mean is μ. In other words, as the sample size increases, the distribution will behave normally.

Estimating Parameters

A point estimate of a population parameter is a single statistic. For example, the sample mean is a point estimate of the population mean. Once all calculations are made, a confidence interval is used to express the accuracy of the sampling method used. The confidence interval consists of a confidence level, the statistic, and a margin of error. A 95% confidence level indicates that 95% of all confidence intervals will contain the population parameter. Also, the margin of error gives a range of values above and below the sample statistic, which helps to form a confidence interval.

The Principles of Hypotheses Testing

The *P*-value approach to hypothesis testing involves assuming a null hypothesis is true and then determining the probability of a test statistic in the direction of the alternative hypothesis. The test statistic is defined as the *t*-statistic $t^* = \frac{\bar{x}-\mu}{s/\sqrt{n}}$, which follows a *t*-distribution with *n*-1 degrees of freedom. The *P*-value is then calculated as the probability that if the null hypothesis is true, a more extreme test statistic in the direction of the alternative hypothesis would be observed. A significance level, α, is set (usually at 0.05 or 0.001) and the *P*-value is compared to α. If $P \leq \alpha$, one rejects the null hypothesis and accepts the alternative hypothesis. If $P > \alpha$, one accepts the null hypothesis.

Measuring Probabilities with Two-Way Frequency Tables

When measuring event probabilities, two-way frequency tables can be used to report the raw data and then used to calculate probabilities. If the frequency tables are translated into relative frequency tables, the probabilities presented in the table can be plugged directly into the formulas for conditional probabilities. By plugging in the correct frequencies, the data from the table can be used to determine if events are independent or dependent.

Differing Probabilities

The probability that event A occurs differs from the probability that event A occurs given B. When working within a given model, it's important to note the difference. $P(A|B)$ is determined using the formula $P(A|B) = \frac{P\ (A \text{ and } B)}{P(B)}$ and represents the total number of A's outcomes left that could occur after B occurs. $P(A)$ can be calculated without any regard for B. For example, the probability of a student finding a parking spot on a busy campus is different once class is in session.

Uniform and Non-Uniform Probability Models

A *uniform probability model* is one where each outcome has an equal chance of occurring, such as the probabilities of rolling each side of a die. A *non-uniform probability model* is one where each outcome has an unequal chance of occurring. In a uniform probability model, the conditional probability formulas for $P(B|A)$ and $P(A|B)$ can be multiplied by their respective denominators to obtain two formulas for $P(A \text{ and } B)$. Therefore, the multiplication rule is derived as $P(A \text{ and } B) = P(A)P(B|A) = P(B)P(A|B)$. In a model, if the probability of either individual event is known and the corresponding conditional probability is known, the multiplication rule allows the probability of the joint occurrence of A and B to be calculated.

Binomial Experiments

In statistics, a *binomial experiment* is an experiment that has the following properties. The experiment consists of *n* repeated trial that can each have only one of two outcomes. It can be either a success or a failure. The probability of success, *p*, is the same in every trial. Each trial is also independent of all other trials. An example of a binomial experiment is rolling a die 10 times with the goal of rolling a 5. Rolling a 5 is a success while any other value is a failure. In this experiment, the probability of rolling a 5 is $\frac{1}{6}$. In any binomial experiment, x is the number of resulting successes, n is the number of trials, p is the probability of success in each trial, and $q = 1 - p$ is the probability of failure within each trial. The probability of obtaining x successes within n trials is:

$$P(X = x) = \frac{n!}{x!\,(n - x)!} p^x (1 - p)^{n-x}$$

With the following being the *binomial coefficient*:

$$\binom{n}{x} = \frac{n!}{x!\,(n - x)!}$$

Within this calculation, $n!$ is n factorial that's defined as:

$$n \cdot (n - 1) \cdot (n - 2) \ldots 1$$

Let's look at the probability of obtaining 2 rolls of a 5 out of the 10 rolls.

Start with $P(X = 2)$, where 2 is the number of successes. Then fill in the rest of the formula with what is known, *n*=10, *x*=2, *p*=1/6, *q*=5/6:

$$P(X = 2) = \left(\frac{10!}{2!\,(10 - 2)!}\right)\left(\frac{1}{6}\right)^2 \left(1 - \frac{1}{6}\right)^{10-2}$$

Which simplifies to:

$$P(X = 2) = \left(\frac{10!}{2!\,8!}\right)\left(\frac{1}{6}\right)^2 \left(\frac{5}{6}\right)^8$$

Then solve to get:

$$P(X = 2) = \left(\frac{3628800}{80640}\right)(.0277)(.2325) = .2898$$

Measurement Scales

There are four types of scales used in mathematics and statistics to standardize measurements: nominal, ordinal, interval, and ratio. A nominal scale is not a measurement; rather, it replaces labels or categories with numbers. To track people's political affiliations, a researcher might assign Republicans the number one, Democrats the number two, Libertarians the number three, and so on. This is an example of a nominal scale. An ordinal scale places items in order from least to greatest or greatest to least, but the distance or interval between each item is unknown. Contests use the ordinal scale. In a science fair, students might be ranked in first, second, or third place, but they wouldn't know how much *better* first was from second and so forth. An interval includes the order and the distance between each item. It lacks an absolute zero; in other words, a complete absence of whatever it is you're measuring. The Fahrenheit Scale is an excellent example. Someone might understand that forty degrees Fahrenheit is twice as hot as twenty, but, at the same, there's no true zero, where it can't get any colder. Lastly, is the ratio scale. Ratio scales can be ranked from least to greatest or greatest to least, the order and the distance between each item is known, and ratio scales include an absolute zero, or the absence of whatever is being measured. Body weight is a common example of something measured on a ratio scale. When someone steps on a scale, he or she knows that one hundred pounds is exactly twice as much as fifty, and when that person steps off the scale, the needle jumps back to zero, indicating a complete absence of weight.

Interpreting Displays of Data

A set of data can be visually displayed in various forms allowing for quick identification of characteristics of the set. Histograms, such as the one shown below, display the number of data points (vertical axis) that fall into given intervals (horizontal axis) across the range of the set. The histogram below displays the heights of black cherry trees in a certain city park. Each rectangle represents the number of trees with heights between a given five-point span. For example, the furthest bar to the right indicates that two trees are between 85 and 90 feet. Histograms can describe the center, spread, shape, and any unusual characteristics of a data set.

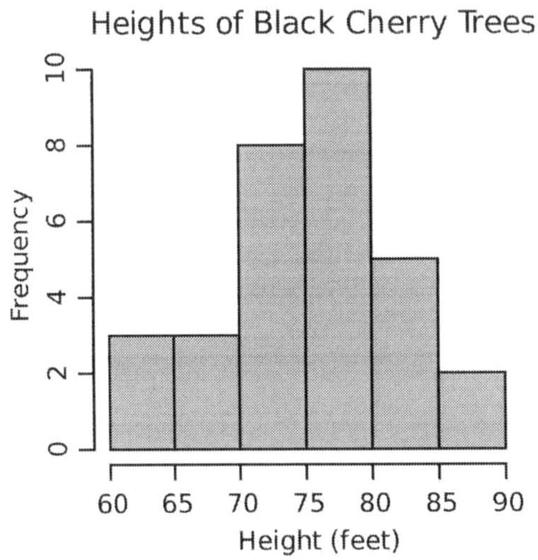

A box plot, also called a box-and-whisker plot, divides the data points into four groups and displays the five-number summary for the set, as well as any outliers. The five-number summary consists of:

- The lower extreme: the lowest value that is not an outlier
- The higher extreme: the highest value that is not an outlier
- The median of the set: also referred to as the second quartile or Q_2
- The first quartile or Q_1: the median of values below Q_2
- The third quartile or Q_3: the median of values above Q_2

To construct a box (or box-and-whisker) plot, the five-number summary for the data set is calculated as follows: the second quartile (Q_2) is the median of the set. The first quartile (Q_1) is the median of the values below Q_2. The third quartile (Q_3) is the median of the values above Q_2. The upper extreme is the highest value in the data set if it is not an outlier (greater than 1.5 times the interquartile range Q_3 - Q_1). The lower extreme is the least value in the data set if it is not an outlier (more than 1.5 times lower than the interquartile range). To construct the box-and-whisker plot, each value is plotted on a number line, along with any outliers. The box consists of Q_1 and Q_3 as its top and bottom and Q_2 as the dividing line inside the box. The whiskers extend from the lower extreme to Q_1 and from Q_3 to the upper extreme.

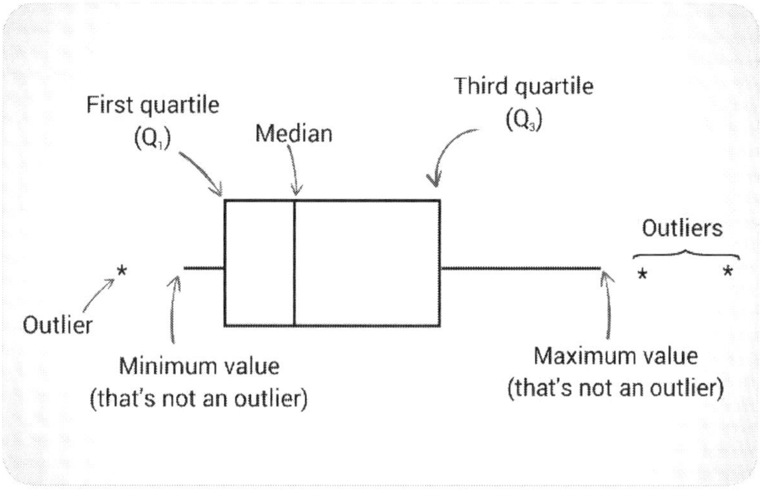

Suppose the box plot displays IQ scores for 12th grade students at a given school. The five-number summary of the data consists of: lower extreme (67); upper extreme (127); Q_2or median (100); Q_1 (91); Q_3 (108); and outliers (135 and 140). Although all data points are not known from the plot, the points are divided into four quartiles each, including 25% of the data points. Therefore, 25% of students scored between 67 and 91, 25% scored between 91 and 100, 25% scored between 100 and 108, and 25% scored between 108 and 127. These percentages include the normal values for the set and exclude the outliers. This information is useful when comparing a given score with the rest of the scores in the set.

A scatter plot is a mathematical diagram that visually displays the relationship or connection between two variables. The independent variable is placed on the *x*-axis, or horizontal axis, and the dependent variable is placed on the *y*-axis, or vertical axis. When visually examining the points on the graph, if the points model a linear relationship, or a line of best-fit can be drawn through the points with the points relatively close on either side, then a correlation exists. If the line of best-fit has a positive slope (rises from left to right), then the variables have a positive correlation. If the line of best-fit has a negative slope (falls from left to right), then the variables have a negative correlation. If a line of best-fit cannot be drawn, then no correlation exists. A positive or negative correlation can be categorized as strong or weak, depending on how closely the points are graphed around the line of best-fit.

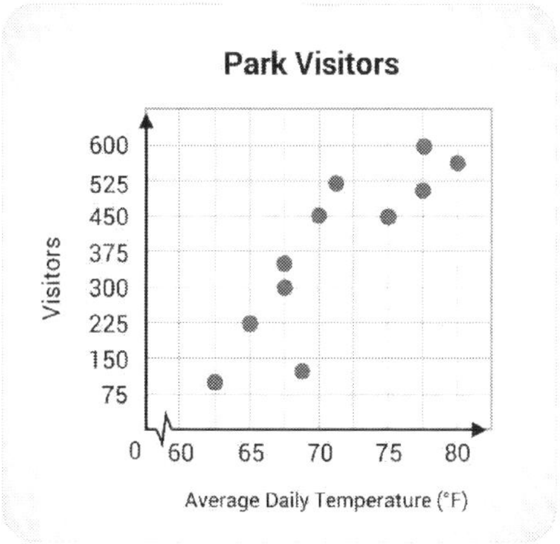

Graphical Representation of Data

Like a scatter plot, a line graph compares variables that change continuously, typically over time. Paired data values (ordered pair) are plotted on a coordinate grid with the *x*- and *y*-axis representing the variables. A line is drawn from each point to the next, going from left to right. The line graph below displays cell phone use for given years (two variables) for men, women, and both sexes (three data sets).

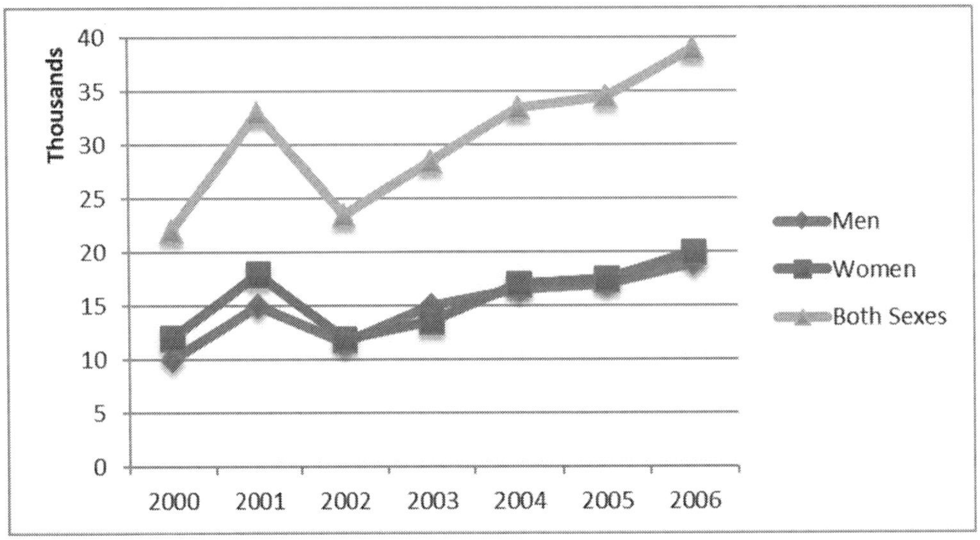

A line plot, also called dot plot, displays the frequency of data (numerical values) on a number line. To construct a line plot, a number line is used that includes all unique data values. It is marked with x's or dots above the value the number of times that the value occurs in the data set. The line plot shown below indicates the number of hours spent playing video games for each day of the week. The first day there were zero hours, the second day there were 2 hours, and so on.

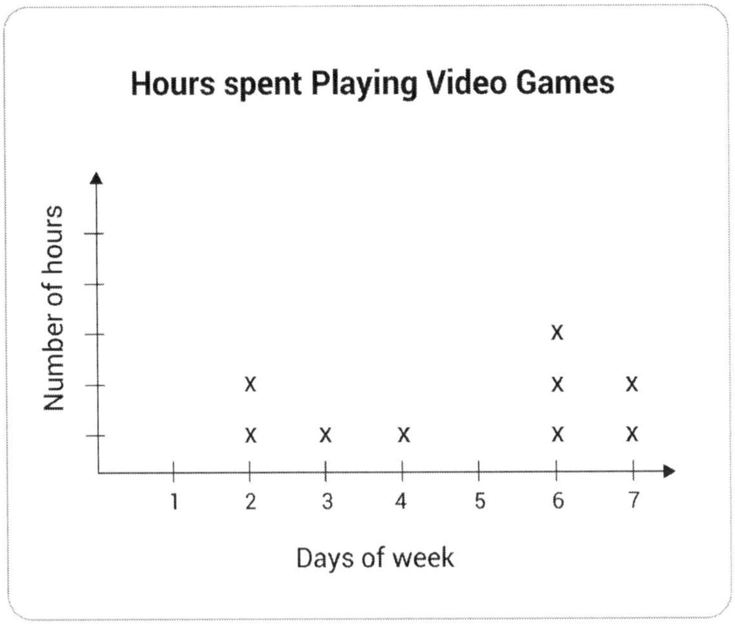

A bar graph looks similar to a histogram but displays categorical data. The horizontal axis represents each category and the vertical axis represents the frequency for the category. A bar is drawn for each category (often different colors) with a height extending to the frequency for that category within the data set. A double bar graph displays two sets of data that contain data points consisting of the same categories. The double bar graph below indicates that two girls and four boys like Pad Thai the most out of all the foods, two boys and five girls like pizza, and so on.

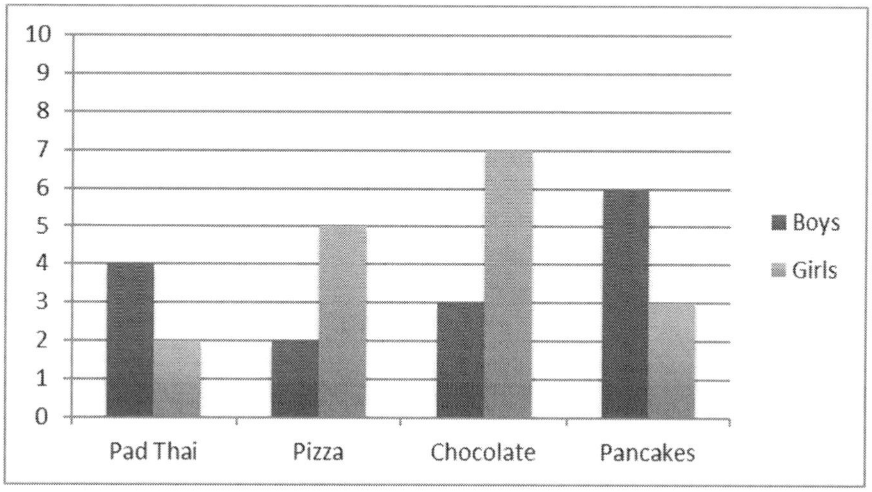

A circle graph, also called a pie chart, displays categorical data with each category representing a percentage of the whole data set. To construct a circle graph, the percent of the data set for each category must be determined. To do so, the frequency of the category is divided by the total number of data points and converted to a percent. For example, if 80 people were asked their favorite pizza topping and 20 responded cheese, then cheese constitutes 25% of the data ($\frac{20}{80} = .25 = 25\%$). Each category in a data set is represented by a *slice* of the circle proportionate to its percentage of the whole.

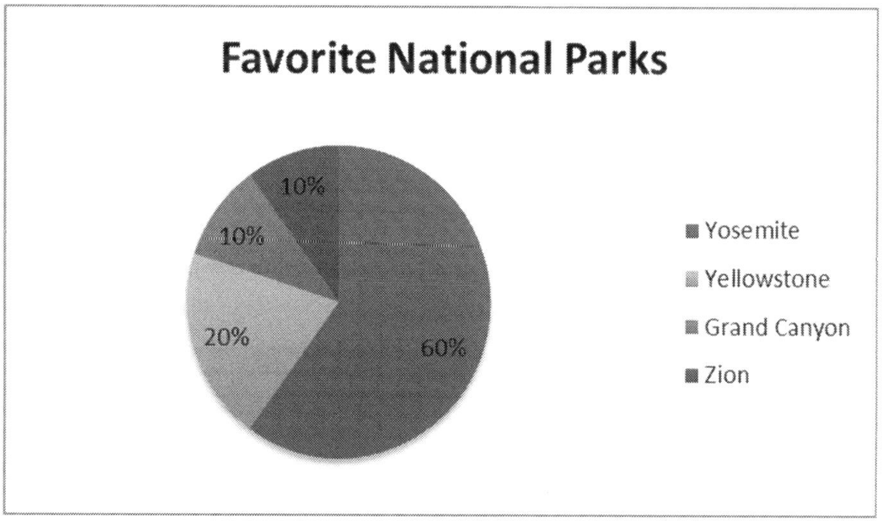

Choice of Graphs to Display Data

Choosing the appropriate graph to display a data set depends on what type of data is included in the set and what information must be displayed. Histograms and box plots can be used for data sets consisting of individual values across a wide range. Examples include test scores and incomes. Histograms and box plots will indicate the center, spread, range, and outliers of a data set. A histogram will show the shape of the data set, while a box plot will divide the set into quartiles (25% increments), allowing for comparison between a given value and the entire set.

Scatter plots and line graphs can be used to display data consisting of two variables. Examples include height and weight, or distance and time. A correlation between the variables is determined by examining the points on the graph. Line graphs are used if each value for one variable pairs with a distinct value for the other variable. Line graphs show relationships between variables.

Line plots, bar graphs, and circle graphs are all used to display categorical data, such as surveys. Line plots and bar graphs both indicate the frequency of each category within the data set. A line plot is used when the categories consist of numerical values. For example, the number of hours of TV watched by individuals is displayed on a line plot. A bar graph is used when the categories consists of words. For example, the favorite ice cream of individuals is displayed with a bar graph. A circle graph can be used to display either type of categorical data. However, unlike line plots and bar graphs, a circle graph does not indicate the frequency of each category. Instead, the circle graph represents each category as its percentage of the whole data set.

Probabilities

Given a set of possible outcomes *X*, a *probability distribution* on *X* is a function that assigns a probability to each possible outcome. If the outcomes are $(x_1, x_2, x_3, \dots x_n)$, and the probability distribution is *p*, then the following rules are applied.

- $0 \leq p(x_i) \leq 1$, for any i.
- $\sum_{i=1}^{n} p(x_i) = 1$.

In other words, the probability of a given outcome must be between zero and 1, while the total probability must be 1.

If $p(x_i)$ is constant, then this is called a *uniform probability distribution*, and $p(x_i) = \frac{1}{n}$. For example, on a six-sided die, the probability of each of the six outcomes will be $\frac{1}{6}$.

If seeking the probability of an outcome occurring in some specific range *A* of possible outcomes, written $P(A)$, add up the probabilities for each outcome in that range. For example, consider a six-sided die, and figure the probability of getting a 3 or lower when it is rolled. The possible rolls are 1, 2, 3, 4, 5, and 6. So, to get a 3 or lower, a roll of 1, 2, or 3 must be completed. The probabilities of each of these is $\frac{1}{6}$, so add these to get $p(1) + p(2) + p(3) = \frac{1}{6} + \frac{1}{6} + \frac{1}{6} = \frac{1}{2}$.

Conditional Probabilities

An outcome occasionally lies within some range of possibilities *B*, and the probability that the outcomes also lie within some set of possibilities *A* needs to be figured. This is called a *conditional probability*. It is written as $P(A|B)$, which is read "the probability of *A* given *B*." The general formula for computing conditional probabilities is:

$$P(A|B) = \frac{P(A \cap B)}{P(B)}$$

However, when dealing with uniform probability distributions, simplify this a bit. Write $|A|$ to indicate the number of outcomes in *A*. Then, for uniform probability distributions, write $P(A|B) = \frac{|A \cap B|}{|B|}$ (recall that $A \cap B$ means "*A* intersect *B*," and consists of all of the outcomes that lie in both *A* and *B*). This means that all possible outcomes do not need to be known. To see why this formula works, suppose that the set of outcomes *X* is $(x_1, x_2, x_3, \ldots x_n)$, so that $|X| = n$. Then, for a uniform probability distribution, $P(A) = \frac{|A|}{n}$. However, this means:

$$(A|B) = \frac{P(A \cap B)}{P(B)} = \frac{\frac{|A \cap B|}{n}}{\frac{|B|}{n}} = \frac{|A \cap B|}{|B|}$$

since the *n*'s cancel out.

For example, suppose a die is rolled and it is known that it will land between 1 and 4. However, how many sides the die has is unknown. Figure the probability that the die is rolled higher than 2. To figure this, $P(3)$ or $P(4)$ does not need to be determined, or any of the other probabilities, since it is known that a fair die has a uniform probability distribution. Therefore, apply the formula $\frac{|A \cap B|}{|B|}$. So, in this case *B* is (1, 2, 3, 4) and $A \cap B$ is (3, 4). Therefore:

$$\frac{|A \cap B|}{|B|} = \frac{2}{4} = \frac{1}{2}$$

Conditional probability is an important concept because, in many situations, the likelihood of one outcome can differ radically depending on how something else comes out. The probability of passing a test given that one has studied all of the material is generally much higher than the probability of passing a test given that one has not studied at all. The probability of a person having heart trouble is much lower if that person exercises regularly. The probability that a college student will graduate is higher when his or her SAT scores are higher, and so on. For this reason, there are many people who are interested in conditional probabilities.

Note that in some practical situations, changing the order of the conditional probabilities can make the outcome very different. For example, the probability that a person with heart trouble has exercised regularly is quite different than the probability that a person who exercises regularly will have heart trouble. The probability of a person receiving a military-only award, given that he or she is or was a soldier, is generally not very high, but the probability that a person being or having been a soldier, given that he or she received a military-only award, is 1.

However, in some cases, the outcomes do not influence one another this way. If the probability of *A* is the same regardless of whether *B* is given; that is, if $P(A|B) = P(A)$, then *A* and *B* are considered *independent*.

In this case:

$$P(A|B) = \frac{P(A \cap B)}{P(B)} = P(A)$$

so $P(A \cap B) = P(A)P(B)$. In fact, if $P(A \cap B) = P(A)P(B)$, it can be determined that $P(A|B) = P(A)$ and $P(A|B) = P(B)$ by working backward. Therefore, *B* is also independent of *A*.

An example of something being independent can be seen in rolling dice. In this case, consider a red die and a green die. It is expected that when the dice are rolled, the outcome of the green die should not depend in any way on the outcome of the red die. Or, to take another example, if the same die is rolled repeatedly, then the next number rolled should not depend on which numbers have been rolled previously. Similarly, if a coin is flipped, then the next flip's outcome does not depend on the outcomes of previous flips.

This can sometimes be counter-intuitive, since when rolling a die or flipping a coin, there can be a streak of surprising results. If, however, it is known that the die or coin is fair, then these results are just the result of the fact that over long periods of time, it is very likely that some unlikely streaks of outcomes will occur. Therefore, avoid making the mistake of thinking that when considering a series of independent outcomes, a particular outcome is "due to happen" simply because a surprising series of outcomes has already been seen.

There is a second type of common mistake that people tend to make when reasoning about statistical outcomes: the idea that when something of low probability happens, this is surprising. It would be surprising that something with low probability happened after just one attempt. However, with so much happening all at once, it is easy to see at least something happen in a way that seems to have a very low probability. In fact, a lottery is a good example. The odds of winning a lottery are very small, but the odds that somebody wins the lottery each week are actually fairly high. Therefore, no one should be surprised when some low probability things happen.

Practice Questions

1. Two cards are drawn from a shuffled deck of 52 cards. What's the probability that both cards are Kings if the first card isn't replaced after it's drawn and is a King?

   a. $^{1}/_{169}$

   b. $^{1}/_{221}$

   c. $^{1}/_{13}$

   d. $^{4}/_{13}$

   e. $^{1}/_{104}$

2. What's the probability of rolling a 6 at least once in two rolls of a die?

   a. $^{1}/_{3}$

   b. $^{1}/_{36}$

   c. $^{1}/_{6}$

   d. $^{1}/_{12}$

   e. $^{11}/_{36}$

3. Given the set $A = \{1, 2, 3, 4, 5, 6, 7, 8, 9, 10\}$ and $B = \{1, 2, 3, 4, 5\}$,what is $A - (A \cap B)$?
   a. $\{6, 7, 8, 9, 10\}$
   b. $\{1, 2, 3, 4, 5\}$
   c. $\{1, 2, 3, 4, 5, 6, 7, 8, 9, 10\}$
   d. $\emptyset$
   e. $\{-1, -2, -3, -4, -5\}$

4. Given the value of a given stock at monthly intervals, which graph should be used to best represent the trend of the stock?
   a. Box plot
   b. Line plot
   c. Line graph
   d. Circle graph
   e. Dot plot

5. For a group of 20 men, the median weight is 180 pounds and the range is 30 pounds. If each man gains 10 pounds, which of the following would be true?
   a. The median weight will increase, and the range will remain the same.
   b. The median weight and range will both remain the same.
   c. The median weight will stay the same, and the range will increase.
   d. The median weight and range will both increase.
   e. The median weight will increase and the range will decrease.

6. A sample data set contains the following values: 1, 3, 5, 7. What's the standard deviation of the set?
   a. 2.58
   b. 4
   c. 6.23
   d. 1.1
   e. 0.25

7. In a statistical experiment, 29 college students are given an exam during week 11 of the semester, and 30 college students are given an exam during week 12 of the semester. Both groups are being tested to determine which exam week might result in a higher grade. What's the degree of freedom in this experiment?
   a. 29
   b. 30
   c. 59
   d. 28
   e. 23

8. What is the probability of randomly picking the winner and runner-up from a race of 4 horses and distinguishing which is the winner?
   a. $\frac{1}{4}$
   b. $\frac{1}{2}$
   c. $\frac{1}{16}$
   d. $\frac{1}{12}$
   e. $\frac{1}{64}$

9. What is the interquartile range (IQR) of the following data set? 1, 4, 6, 6, 9, 10, 12, 17, 18
   a. 10
   b. 9
   c. 14.5
   d. 5
   e. 9.5

$$G = .035O + .26$$

10. The linear regression model above is based on an analysis of the price of a gallon of gas (G) at 15 gas stations compared to the price of a barrel of oil (O) at the time. Based on this model, which of the following statements are true?

I. There is a negative correlation between G and O.

II. When oil is \$55 per barrel then gas is approximately \$2.19 per gallon.

III. The slope of the line indicates that as O increases by 1, G increases by .035.

IV. If the price of oil increases by \$8 per barrel then the price of gas will increase by approximately \$0.18 per gallon.

a. I and II

b. II only

c. II and III

d. I and III

e. II, III, and IV

Answer Explanations

1. B: For the first card drawn, the probability of a King being pulled is $^4/_{52}$. Since this card isn't replaced, if a King is drawn first, the probability of a King being drawn second is $^3/_{51}$. The probability of a King being drawn in both the first and second draw is the product of the two probabilities: $^4/_{52}$ x $^3/_{51}$= $^{12}/_{2652}$ which, divided by 12, equals $^1/_{221}$.

2. E: The addition rule is necessary to determine the probability because a 6 can be rolled on either roll of the die. The rule used is $P(A \text{ or } B) = P(A) + P(B) - P(A \text{ and } B)$. The probability of a 6 being individually rolled is $^1/_6$ and the probability of a 6 being rolled twice is $^1/_6 \cdot {}^1/_6 = {}^1/_{36}$. Therefore, the probability that a 6 is rolled at least once is $1/6 + 1/6 - 1/36 = 11/36$

3. A: $(A \cap B)$ is equal to the intersection of the two sets A and B, which is $\{1, 2, 3, 4, 5\}$. $A - (A \cap B)$ is equal to the elements of A that are *not* included in the set $(A \cap B)$. Therefore, $A - (A \cap B) = \{6, 7, 8, 9, 10\}$.

4. C: The scenario involves data consisting of two variables: month and stock value. Box plots display data consisting of values for one variable. Therefore, a box plot is not an appropriate choice. Both line plots (which are also called dot plots) and circle graphs are used to display frequencies within categorical data. Neither can be used for the given scenario. Line graphs display two numerical variables on a coordinate grid and show trends among the variables, so this is the correct choice.

5. A: If each man gains 10 pounds, every original data point will increase by 10 pounds. Therefore, the man with the original median will still have the median value, but that value will increase by 10. The smallest value and largest value will also increase by 10 and, therefore, the difference between the two won't change. The range does not change in value and, thus, remains the same.

6. A: First, the sample mean must be calculated. $\bar{x} = \frac{1}{4}(1 + 3 + 5 + 7) = 4$. The standard deviation of the data set is:

$$\sigma = \sqrt{\frac{\sum(x - \bar{x})^2}{n - 1}}$$

and $n = 4$ represents the number of data points. Therefore:

$$\sigma = \sqrt{\frac{1}{3}[(1 - 4)^2 + (3 - 4)^2 + (5 - 4)^2 + (7 - 4)^2]}$$

$$\sqrt{\frac{1}{3}(9 + 1 + 1 + 9)} = 2.58$$

7. E: The degree of freedom for two samples is calculated as:

$$df = \frac{(n_1 - 1) + (n_2 - 1)}{2}$$

rounded to the lowest whole number. For this example:

$$df = \frac{(29 - 1) + (30 - 1)}{2} = \frac{28 + 29}{2} = 28.5$$

which, rounded to the lowest whole number, is 28.

8. D: The probability of picking the winner of the race is $\frac{1}{4}\left(\frac{number\ of\ favorable\ outcomes}{number\ of\ total\ outcomes}\right)$. Assuming the winner was picked on the first selection, three horses remain from which to choose the runner-up (these are dependent events). Therefore, the probability of picking the runner-up is $\frac{1}{3}$. To determine the probability of multiple events, the probability of each event is multiplied: $\frac{1}{4} \times \frac{1}{3} = \frac{1}{12}$.

9. E: The interquartile range (IQR) is the difference between the value of the 75th percentile and the 25th percentile of a data set, or the third and first quartiles. The first step in calculating the IQR is to arrange the numbers in the data set from lowest to highest value, as they are in this problem. When the number of data points in the set is odd (as it is in this problem), the median, which is the second quartile, is not included in the upper and lower quartiles. The remaining data points are then divided into two equal groups. Then, the median of both of these groups is found, remembering that the median is the average of the two middle points if the number of values is even, as it is in this case, with four numbers. The median of the upper group is the upper quartile and the median of the lower group is the lower quartile. Finally, the IQR is calculated as the difference between the median of the upper quartile and that of the lower quartile.

So, for this problem, the data set provided was: 1, 4, 6, 6, 9, 10, 12, 17, 18.

There are nine values, so the median (9) is excluded. This makes the lower group 1, 4, 6, and 6. Then the upper group is 10, 12, 17, and 18. The median of the lower group is 5 (the average of 4 and 6) and the median of the upper group is 14.5 (the average of 12 and 17).

Thus, the IQR is 14.5 — 5 = 9.5.

10. C: II and III are the only true statements. If graphed this line would have a positive correlation, which make statement I false. Also, if the price of oil increases by $8 per barrel then gas price would increase by $.035(8) = \$0.28$ per gallon. This make statement IV false as well.

Photo Credits

"Black cherry tree histogram" by Mwtoews
(https://commons.wikimedia.org/wiki/Histogram#/media/File:Black_cherry_tree_histogram.svg)

Dear SAT Math 1 Test Taker,

We would like to start by thanking you for purchasing this study guide for your SAT Math 1 exam. We hope that we exceeded your expectations.

Our goal in creating this study guide was to cover all of the topics that you will see on the test. We also strove to make our practice questions as similar as possible to what you will encounter on test day. With that being said, if you found something that you feel was not up to your standards, please send us an email and let us know.

We would also like to let you know about other books in our catalog that may interest you.

SAT Math 2

This can be found on Amazon: amazon.com/dp/1628454725

SAT Biology

amazon.com/dp/1628454806

SAT

amazon.com/dp/1628455217

ACCUPLACER

amazon.com/dp/162845492X

AP Biology

amazon.com/dp/1628454989

We have study guides in a wide variety of fields. If the one you are looking for isn't listed above, then try searching for it on Amazon or send us an email.

Thanks Again and Happy Testing!
Product Development Team
info@studyguideteam.com

Interested in buying more than 10 copies of our product? Contact us about bulk discounts:

bulkorders@studyguideteam.com

FREE Test Taking Tips DVD Offer

To help us better serve you, we have developed a Test Taking Tips DVD that we would like to give you for FREE. **This DVD covers world-class test taking tips that you can use to be even more successful when you are taking your test.**

All that we ask is that you email us your feedback about your study guide. Please let us know what you thought about it – whether that is good, bad or indifferent.

To get your **FREE Test Taking Tips DVD**, email freedvd@studyguideteam.com with "FREE DVD" in the subject line and the following information in the body of the email:

a. The title of your study guide.

b. Your product rating on a scale of 1-5, with 5 being the highest rating.

c. Your feedback about the study guide. What did you think of it?

d. Your full name and shipping address to send your free DVD.

If you have any questions or concerns, please don't hesitate to contact us at freedvd@studyguideteam.com.

Thanks again!

61004860R00066

Made in the USA
Middletown, DE
17 August 2019